The Complete Book
of Golf Games

Also by the author

The Complete Book of Beer Drinking Games

Beer Games 2: The Exploitative Sequel

THE COMPLETE BOOK OF

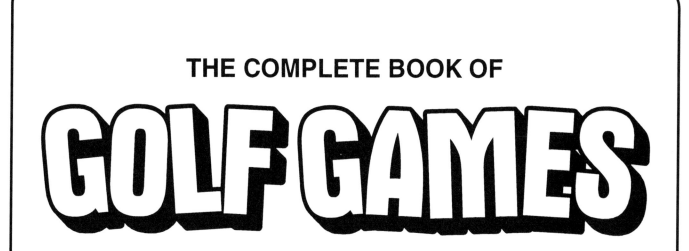

GOLF GAMES

Scott Johnston

Illustrations by Joe Kohl

Mustang Publishing
Memphis, TN

Library of Congress Cataloging-in-Publication Data
Johnston, Scott, 1960-
    The complete book of golf games / Scott Johnston; illustrations by Joe Kohl.
        p.   cm.
    ISBN 0-914457-55-1 (pbk. : alk. paper)
    1. Golf–Betting. 2. Wagers. 3. Games. I. Title.
  GV979.B47J64   1995
  796.352'6–dc20   95-2890
                                          CIP
                                          Rev.

Printed on acid-free paper.
10 9 8 7 6 5 4 3 2

For my father

Acknowledgments

My sincere thanks to the following collaborators and co-conspirators: my father George, Chip Oat, Doc-oh! Burke, Jim "Cajun Man" Hansen, Jim McLean (for reducing my handicap and contributing a few games), Dave Eaton, Gary "Buddha" Griffith, Bill Black, Mike "The Pro" Muller, the Neoportes, Ted "Big Joe" Berenblum, David Glenz, Anne McDonnell, struggling West Coast entrepreneur and golf benefactor Scott McNealy, my brothers Bart and Bill, Ed Steele, Mike Lopuzinski, Dave Mahoney, Allen Quarterman, Dave "Sandbag" Wasson, Tommy Kelly, Joe Kohl, Clair Stamatien, Mark Harris, Rollin Riggs, plus Dave Tohir and Mark Graham (if only because I play a lot of golf with them).

Scott Johnston

Contents

Confessions of a Convert

L IKE MOST OBSESSIONS, golf is understood only by the obsessed. Generations of perplexed golf widows can offer weary testimony to the game's singular allure — an allure that borders on mysticism. A friend of mine calls it the "Inner Truth." I myself once lacked the Inner Truth.

Growing up, I lived a stone's throw from three of the world's finest courses. I could have played them whenever I wanted — an opportunity that would tempt most golfers to consign their firstborn to an eternal damnation of tennis lessons. I could have, but I didn't. In fact, I didn't care for golf at all. Baseball and body-surfing were my passions, tennis an occasional diversion.

To me, golf was a once-a-year chore. Toward the end of each summer, I would reluctantly but dutifully drag myself from the tennis court or the beach (God forbid surf was up!) and make a cameo appearance at the club's Father-Son Golf Tournament. Despite the club-maximum 36 strokes I was given, my dad and I never did very well.

The way I saw it, golf had the following problems:

- It took *way* too long.
- It offered no exercise.
- It was too damn hard.

I readily produced these gripes when I needed to bring my golfing friends down a notch, when I wanted to suggest that my sports were superior. Heck, most people don't even call golf a sport; it's a *game*, right?

This observation, I was sure, twisted a rusty sand wedge into the collective gut of golfers everywhere.

Oddly, I could never ruffle their feathers. My golfing pals always maintained a graceful calm that I couldn't penetrate (see *Golf in the Kingdom*). Often, the bastards wouldn't even fight back. It was like arguing with that guy on *Kung Fu*: you thought you had the last word, but his mystical serenity always suggested otherwise. (And then he kicked your butt, but that's beside the point.)

I don't remember the precise moment I came to possess the Inner Truth. There was no sudden, "born again" epiphany while walking to work or taking out the garbage. It was more of a gradual revelation over the course of one summer.

The U.S. Open came to town early that season. Though the prospect of watching golf seemed even duller than actually playing, I speculated that the overall "scene" might warrant investigation. One of the players, Bob Tway, was staying at our house. Though he had won the Westchester Classic the week before, I had never heard of Tway. He seemed a likable guy, very soft-spoken. Many of our friends were hosting big stars like Nicklaus and Norman, so suddenly the Open took on serious social significance: it was neighbor versus neighbor. "Was that a 76 your houseguest shot yesterday? Such a pity…"

> **"Golf and sex are the only things you can enjoy without being good at them."**
> **—Jimmy Demaret**

So I followed Tway around, and he became someone to root for. To my surprise, I grew mildly interested in the proceedings, especially as Tway took the lead from time to time. And damned if he didn't almost win the thing. Tway held the lead after the first round and for about five minutes near the end of the fourth. (Ray Floyd got that "stare" of his going and won in a dogfight to the finish.)

Tway's success, though, bestowed great bragging rights upon our household in the trenches of clubs and cocktail parties. More important, I began thinking about golf in a less-than-hostile light.

In the afterglow of the Open, I played one or two lackluster rounds — rekindling memories of my flirtation with chess after the celebrated Fisher/Spassky matches. And, like all the Grand Masters that never were, I might have moved on to other things when the excitement wore off. Except, I hit a few good shots. Not many, but enough. Watching the pros up close for four days was like watching Sybervision with God—something was bound to rub off.

As any golfer knows, all it takes is that one shot, that one sublime moment when you watch your three-iron draw gracefully over the water hazard and roll within two feet of the pin, to bring you back again. *Yeah, that was easy, that was sweet,* you think. *With a little practice, I could do that all the time.*

> **"Golf is a game to teach you about the messages from within, about the subtle voices of the body-mind... Nowhere does a man go so naked."**
> **— Michael Murphy, Golf in the Kingdom**

Willie Nelson once said that there were some golf shots he wouldn't trade for an orgasm. I used to think that was the dumbest thing I had ever heard. But slowly, over the course of a summer, I decided Willie was onto something. I was glimpsing the Inner Truth.

By September, I was playing 18 holes in my head to get to sleep instead of counting sheep. I traded swing thoughts with my friends. I talked knowingly of square grooves, 60-degree wedges, and new "tracks." I even joined a club. I was hooked.

Since then, I have tried desperately to make up for lost time. I threw myself into the game, traveling, taking lessons, imagining that I could someday hit draws and fades at will. I have even had some success, reducing my handicap in successive summers until I leveled off in single digits. And my dad and I finally won that Father-Son Tournament, our last, five months before his death.

In the process, I learned some things:
- Golf does take a long time, but there is perhaps no greater use of it.
- It still isn't any exercise, but who really cares?
- Yes, it is too damn hard.

What I never comprehended—and what the Inner Truth has taught me—was the beauty of golf's tranquility and exquisite frustrations, the fun of its endlessly varying challenges, and, most important, the joy of its fellowship and new friends. To illustrate, try this experiment: Introduce two tennis players to each other. Now introduce two golfers. Who do you think will hit it off? Have you ever seen tennis players cluster at a backyard barbecue?

Golfers have an affinity that dwells on a higher spiritual plane. They are immediate kindred spirits, bonded by tales of impossible ups-and-downs and two-iron fades. Also, I believe, they are just plain nice people.

All this brings me to the point of this book. As well as enjoying golf, I enjoy competition, and I certainly enjoy a good wager. Many golfers spend their whole lives playing routine Nassaus without knowing many of the other fine and amusing ways to lose their money on Saturday morning. And many clubs never have tournaments more clever than Medal Play or Best Ball. Perhaps a Monkey Tournament or a round of String will revive the dead at your club. Thus, in the hope of making golf an even more pleasurable experience—if such a thing is possible—I humbly submit this compendium of betting and tournament formats.

Some games, like Nassaus, are predictable but necessary for a "complete" book. Some are ridiculous, in which case I say so. Some are unusual and creative. And still others are borderline crazy and have little to do with real golf. I was, truth be told, an avid Shoe Golfer years before I cared for the real thing.

Anyway, I hope this book will make your good golf times even better. So swing slow, let it flow, and receive the Inner Truth.

> **"Never bet anyone you meet on the first tee who has a deep suntan, a one-iron in his bag, and squinty eyes."**
> **—Dave Marr**

CHAPTER 1

Games for Twosomes, Threesomes, & Foursomes

Skins

Skins is for the gambler's gambler, the type who thrives on the convergence of money and pressure. Also known as "Scats," Skins has been around for some time, but it has become widely popular thanks to ABC's annual Skins game every Thanksgiving.

So many viewers watch the pros battle in the desert (the Skins game is second only to the Masters in ratings) that the network created the Senior Skins game, too. In 1990, Arnold Palmer made more money on one hole than in any single year in his career. It seems that armchair golfers can't get enough of watching someone sweat over a putt worth $200,000.

Skins is very straightforward. Each "skin" has an assigned value, usually a dollar or two per player. The player who wins a hole gets a skin. The value of a skin can remain constant over 18 holes or increase as the round progresses. Since the stakes tend to accumulate anyway, it seems pointless to increase them, but heck, they do it on TV, so why not?

To win a skin, a player must win a hole outright on a net basis. ("Net," for those of you really new to this, is your score after adjustment for your handicap.) If players tie, the pot carries over to the next hole, which is then played for two skins. If that hole is tied, the pot carries over again, and so

forth. This is how the stakes can really add up.

For example, suppose we have a foursome, and the stakes are $1 per player per hole. On the first hole, Player 1 shoots a three and everyone else shoots four. Player 1 then wins a skin, which is worth $4. But, since one of the four dollars in the pot was his own, he actually nets $3.

On the second hole, players 3 and 4 shoot fours, but the other two shoot a five and a seven. Players 3 and 4 split the pot, right? Wrong. Remember, if two tie, all tie. In this case, the pot ($4) carries over to the third hole, which is now worth $8, or two skins.

In a simple $1 Skins game, the 18th hole theoretically can be worth $72 (net $54). In case you don't have a firm grasp of the obvious, the downside risk is always 18 times the stakes per hole. So $1 Skins isn't necessarily for wimps.

One of the amusing aspects of Skins, other than the truly exquisite opportunities for choking, is the constantly shifting politics. Someone who was your mortal enemy on one hole because he sunk a ten-foot putt to rob you of three skins becomes your blood brother on the next because you're out of the hole and he has a four-footer to tie someone else and carry the skin over.

Skins is recommended for threesomes and foursomes. (Should your club allow occasional off-hour shenanigans, Skins is also perfect for fivesomes and sixsomes.) I also suggest that you adjust handicaps down either one-third or one-half. Full handicaps tends to give high-handicappers too much of an advantage in this format, since one lucky hole can give them a huge pot.

"They Shoot Slow Golfers, Don't They?"

Golf Magazine determined that Bernhard Langer is the slowest player in professional golf, with an average of 90 seconds per putt. That means the poor guys playing with Bernhard must spend about 50 minutes of their day watching him stalk his putts. As Lanny Wadkins, one of the fastest players on the tour, commented, "I've seen turtles move faster than Bernhard."

In his defense, Bernhard has quickened his pace the last few years, over which time his game has improved. Coincidence?

Incidentally, the fastest putter on the tour—assuming he *is* on tour when you read this—is currently John Daly, who averages about 20 seconds per putt.

Nassau

Undoubtedly golf's most popular wagering format, Nassau originated at the Nassau Country Club on Long Island around 1900 (not in the Bahamas, as many believe). Apparently, the club's team routinely defeated its opponents so easily that a new system of play had to be created. Thus, they decided to award one point for winning the front nine, one point for the back nine, and one point for the match. Today, the "Two Dollar Nassau" now seems as old as golf itself, although we know better.

A modern Nassau is similar to the 1900 version, dividing the wagering into three parts: the front nine, the back nine, and the 18. Teams of two or singles agree on stakes for each segment. Generally, each nine is worth the same amount, and the match is worth either the same or double each nine. (Doubling the back nine but not the match is known as "Four Ways." Another variation—doubling the back nine and tripling the match—is known as "Six Ways.")

If someone on the first tee asks you, "Five, five, and five?" what he means is, "Would you like to play a Nassau for $5 on the front nine, $5 on the back nine, and another $5 on the 18?" Use the Match Play format.

As play progresses, if a team falls two holes behind on either the nine or the 18, they may elect to "press" either the remaining nine or 18. Pressing, also known as "rolling the drums," is, in effect, doubling down. In the case of a $5 Nassau, you'll be wagering an additional $5 on the remaining holes.

(If still on the front nine, players generally press the nine rather than the 18.) The other team is obliged to accept the press. The trailing team isn't obligated to press, but let's just say that, where I come from, only complete wusses don't press. (**Note:** Players can agree on the first tee to make presses automatic whenever a team is two down.)

Further, if a team is down two holes on a press, the press can be pressed as well, and so on.

When one or more presses come into play, scoring can get complicated. If there are two presses, players are competing for four different matches simultaneously. The scorecard can get messy, so pick someone reliable to keep track of everything. He should mark a "P" or a small dot on the card at each hole where a press was called.

Play with full handicaps off the lowest handicap. ▮

Pick Up Sticks

Pick Up Sticks requires some strategy other than just playing good golf. It's also quite entertaining.

For each hole a player loses (play is match play), he may take one club in his opponent's bag out of play. The opponent may reclaim his clubs one at a time, in any order he wants, as he loses holes back. Half-handicaps should be used.

Players should decide before the match whether they can take away putters. Most choose to give the putter immunity, because it's too much of a handicap not to have one. Accomplished players can work around the absence of other clubs by choking up, hitting fades, and so forth, but it's almost comical not to have a putter.

> **"What do I like about golf? It's certainly not the low scores."**
> **–Huey Lewis**

I don't agree, though. You can putt pretty well with a sand wedge or a one- or two-iron. Fuzzy Zoeller once broke his putter in a temper tantrum, and he was forced to finish his round using a wedge for a putter, since PGA rules prohibit club replacement. And Ben Crenshaw once finished a round by putting with his two-iron.

In any event, assuming the putter gets immunity, what are the best clubs to take from your opponent? Though many golfers immediately pick the driver, it's probably the worst club to select. You'd be doing most players a favor by making them tee off with a three-wood or a two-iron. Obviously, a lot depends on your opponent's strengths and weaknesses, as well as the specific challenges of the holes immediately ahead. In general, the sand wedge is the best club to take away. Many good players use it for nearly every shot inside 100 yards. Also, it's tough to recover from greenside bunkers using any club but a sand wedge. On the other hand, if the player carries a lob wedge, taking his sand wedge won't matter much.

A variation of this game is not to use "stroke" handicaps at all but instead have a club handicap from the start. The suggested method is for the higher-handicapped player to remove one club from his opponent's bag for every two strokes in their handicap differential. So if player A has an eight-handicap, and player B has a 14, player B can remove three clubs from player A's bag. The game then progresses in the same manner described above, with clubs coming in and out of play with won and lost holes.

Pick Up Sticks may seem a silly game, but I highly recommend it for beginners. Many of the golf greats learned to play with incomplete bags. The game forces you to create shots, such as "punch fading" a four-iron to hit it as far as a six, or hitting a "running hook" with a six to send it as far as a four. We all tend to get lazy, carrying specialty clubs for every possible lie (yes, I mean you with the "Divine Nine"), so Pick Up Sticks is a healthy and fun diversion. 🏌

GolFact

What was the greatest golf shot during the 1980's? According to a reader's poll conducted by a British magazine, Sandy Lyle's fairway bunker shot on the 18th hole of the Masters in 1988 takes that honor. Lyle hit a seven-iron over a high lip to about 25 feet above the hole. Spin and the slope of the green brought the ball to within ten feet of the pin. Lyle sank the putt to seal his tournament victory.

Bingo Bango Bongo

Bingo Bango Bongo, also known as "Bingle Bangle Bungle," is a fine game that seems to have been largely forgotten. Its format puts separate values on a player's long game, short game, and putting game.

Each hole has three points available. Players may assign any dollar value they wish to each point. The first point goes to the player hitting the green in the fewest strokes. (Fringes don't count, and ties are a half-point each.) The second point goes to the player closest to pin after everyone is on the green (regardless of how many strokes it took to get there). The last point goes to the player in the hole in the fewest strokes. Handicaps can be used, but they only apply to the last point.

Some players award the last point to the first ball in the hole, regardless of the number of strokes. I'm not fond of this version, because it encourages a player who is otherwise out of a hole to lag one or more putts to the point where he's just beyond the range of the other players, thus giving himself the best shot at the final point. (Playing in turn, instead of according to who's away, can defeat this strategy, but that just gets you back to the "low score" approach.)

On par-three holes, no point is awarded for the first ball on the green. Instead, the first point goes to the player who is second-closest to the pin after everyone is on the green.

Bingo Bango Bongo is a good game to play when a foursome has a wide range of handicaps, because the format acts as an equalizer. High handicappers can come out quite well if they have good games around the green and score well relative to their handicaps. Players not adept at hitting greens in regulation, for example, will have a better shot at winning the second point if they are good chippers or bunker players. 🏌

> ## "Miss a putt for $2,000? Not likely!"—Walter Hagen

Snake

A putting game, Snake can be either the central focus of the match or a fun side bet.

The object of the game is not to three-putt. The first player who three-putts holds the "snake." Now, unless you're a member of an obscure Appalachian religious sect, a snake is not something you want to hold. The three-putter must hold the snake until there's another three-putt, at which point the first player hands the snake to someone else (assuming he himself did not three-putt, in which case he keeps it).

Whoever is holding the snake at the end of the ninth and eighteenth holes loses and must pay the others an agreed-upon amount. If this isn't enough action for your blood, try playing in six-hole increments. Some even play one hole at a time, but this is a bit distracting, in my opinion.

Snake is entertaining but slow, since players must putt everything out. You should probably avoid this game when the course is crowded. Endlessly analyzing a three-foot putt is a sure way to annoy the players behind you and get officious course marshals on your back.

Another problem: occasionally a player who has already taken five strokes and still isn't on the green will lay the ball up, sometimes hitting around the green, until he's in an ideal putting position. Playing with such a lowlife will try your patience for Snake, but a large amount of heckling usually solves this problem. ▰●

Yardages

Also known as "Long Holes," Yardages awards points based on the length of each hole, usually one point per yard. A 412-yard hole, for example, is worth 412 points. Par is irrelevant.

Obviously, the longer holes are more important. At the end of the match, add up all the points. Stroke handicaps aren't used, although players can agree to give the higher handicaps some yards up front.

The winner receives either a fixed amount or a specified amount per point. A nickel a point is common. Think twice (or be very confident) before you blurt out, "How about a dollar a yard, gang?" In the example

below, you can see that a mere "nickel round" can add up:

Player	Yards Won	Net Win/(Loss)
1	2,850	$59.60
2	1,670	1.50
3	1,240	-20.90
4	870	-39.40

Yardages is amusing, but only as an occasional diversion. ◗

Wolf

Also called "Wolfman," Wolf is a three-player game. The golfer with the middle-distance drive, regardless of where it lands, is the "wolf." His opponents are the "hunters." The wolf must match twice his net score on the hole against the combined net scores of the hunters. If the amount wagered on each hole is a dollar, the wolf puts up two dollars against one each for the hunters. If the wolf wins, he collects two dollars, whereas the hunters get only one each.

On par-three holes, the wolf is the second-closest to the pin after the first shot.

If there's a tie, players decide whether the stakes carry to the next hole. Any amount carried over goes to the next winning "team," whether it's the wolf or the hunters. Carryovers make Wolf a more interesting game. Large pots make it advantageous to be the wolf, because the wolf doesn't split the pot. Thus, strategy off the tee becomes important, and players will jockey to become the wolf. Honor off the tee is established by the net score on the previous hole. Play with full handicaps. ◗

Lone Wolf

A game for four players, Lone Wolf is a highly recommended alternative to the standard Nassau. On each tee, one player is the designated "wolf" who tees off first. As the wolf watches the others tee off, he may pick any player as his partner on that hole. To choose a player, however, he must select that player immediately after the tee shot (i.e., before anyone else hits). If the wolf still hasn't picked anyone after the last player drives, he must either pick the last player or declare himself the hole: each of the other players bets two units, and the Lone Wolf matches each, for a total of six units. If there's a tie, the units carry over to the next hole. If there's a tie on a Lone Wolf hole, carry two units each so that the Lone Wolf doesn't carry all six units. Carryovers are not doubled when someone elects to be Lone Wolf, unless you're a bunch of animals and you really want to.

The stakes can add up quickly, so there's a lot of strategy involved. You'll uncover several layers of it as you play the game. For instance, if you're the wolf and you hit a poor drive, do you hold out for the best golfer, even if he's up last? What if he slices it into the drink? You might then be forced to take him, just to share your losses.

The position of wolf rotates each hole. Watch to see who strokes on each hole, as this plays a crucial role in partner selection. After 16 holes, every-

"Lone Wolf" and play against everyone else. The other players should greet a decision to be a Lone Wolf with plaintive and theatric howling.

If there's a Lone Wolf, the stakes double for the

one will have been wolf once, so whoever is in last place gets to be the wolf on 17 and 18.

Optional Rule 1: The wolf on any hole may triple the stakes by choosing to become the Lone Wolf after hitting his tee shot but before viewing the other shots. Or, for the really high rollers, the stakes can be quadrupled if the Lone Wolf declares himself prior to any tee shots. This is considered either very brave or very stupid, depending on whom you play with.

Optional Rule 2: When a player is chosen by the wolf to be his partner, he may opt to become the Lone Wolf himself (with stakes doubling, as usual). This effectively "steals" the hole from the wolf. This rule makes each hole's wolf exercise more caution when picking a partner. It also favors better golfers. 🔚

And You Can Bungee Jump after Your Drive...

At Barton Creek in Texas, the 10th hole has a 110-foot drop from the tee to the fairway landing area. Think of it as driving from a 10- or 11-story building. Gives new meaning to the phrase "air it out."

Scotch Foursome (a.k.a. Alternative Shot)

Scotch Foursomes are the most popular gambling format in Great Britain, where it's simply called a "Foursome."

To play, pairs alternate shots from tee to green until the ball is in the hole, although one player should drive all the even holes and the other the odd. Use one-half of combined handicaps.

You must put some thought into who drives which holes. Do the holes that require a good carry tend to be odd or even? Put your long hitter on those tees. Do the par-threes fall on the odds or evens? Put your target hitter on them.

The Scotch Foursome is an excellent game. It really brings a team together, for better or worse. It's also a fast game, as players tend to walk ahead of their partners in a leapfrog fashion. The popularity of this format is one of the main reasons golf is played faster overseas, where a quick pace is *de rigueur*. Most players in the U.S. could use a dose of this mentality. 🔚

Modified Scotch Foursome

In this variation, all players tee off. Partners then decide which ball to play from the second shot. The player whose tee shot is not used hits the third shot. Players alternate from there until the ball is in the hole. Though this format is a fine alternative if players want to try every tee shot, it's much slower than a standard Scotch Foursome. 🏌️

Fairways & Greens

In this game, players receive one unit for each fairway hit in regulation on par-fours and par-fives, and one for each green hit in regulation. Note that there are usually about 24 units per person up for grabs per 18 holes.

Points can be awarded every time a player hits a fairway or a green or can be carried over if two players hit one at the same time (or if all miss). That is, if the entire foursome hits the first fairway, but only one player hits the green, then that player

Some Dumb Records*

Ball Balancing—Lang Martin of Charlotte, North Carolina balanced seven golf balls, one atop of the other, without any adhesive, thus shattering his own record of six.

Ball Bouncing—Mark Mooney of Hummelstown, Pennsylvania bounced a golf ball of the face of a club 1,764 times in 1985. He used a wedge.

Practice Balls—Irving Hemmle of Fort Worth, Texas hit 48,265 practice balls in 1983. It is not known if his handicap improved.

Most Holes in a Year—Ollie Bowers of Gaffney, South Carolina played 9,757 holes in 1969. That's roughly 542 rounds or about 1.5 rounds each day for the entire year. Is this guy married? (Probably.)

Most Holes in 24 Hours—Ian Colston, a professional runner from Australia, played 401 holes in 24 hours. He used a six iron and over 100 miles.

Oldest Player to Shoot His Age—Arthur Thompson of British Columbia, at 103.

Highest Recorded Score for One Round—316 by some French guy in 1888.

*from "Rarities" in *Golf Digest*

earns two points and the others get none.

Fairways & Greens is great for less-experienced golfers because, unlike most golf betting games, it encourages intelligent golf. Narrow fairway? Leave the driver in the bag. Other games, such as Skins, encourage risk-taking that isn't always appropriate for the novice.

On the other hand, no one ever said that smart golf and fun golf are the same thing. 🏌

GolFact

Q: What are the most holes-in-one recorded in a single round?

A: Three, by Dr. Joseph Boydstone of Bakersfield, California (doubtless on a Wednesday afternoon). It has been calculated that the odds of a hole-in-one for an average golfer on an average par-three are 10,331-to-1. That means, assuming that the course didn't have 18 par-three's and that he was an average golfer, Dr. Boydstone beat odds of 4,270,918,224-to-1. To put it differently, a $1.00 bet would have made Dr. Boydstone the richest man in America at the time.

Cross Country

Cross Country is "destination" golf, with the destination being a hole. But only *one* hole.

First, pick a starting point. The first tee is simple, but you can choose anywhere, on or off the course. How about a nearby Wal-Mart? Then pick a hole. The sixth hole? The 12th? Make it the farthest point on the course, if you want. Your mission: get in the hole in as few strokes as possible. Players can choose any route they want, whether on the course or not; there are no boundaries in this game. You'll see your course in a way you've never seen it before.

Where I live, two courses are more or less adjacent to each other. We've played from the first tee of course #1 to the 18th of course #2. (It takes about 35 strokes, in case you're interested.) Be creative. Invent side bets. Can you play from your front yard to your club without being arrested? Can you use public transportation?

Cross Country is, needless to say, an off-hours, even off-season, game.

By the way, in 1963 some knucklehead named

Green-to-Tee

Floyd Rood played the longest Cross Country game ever: the United States, coast-to-coast, starting in California. The course played slightly under six million yards, and Rood shot a 114,737, including penalty shots.

Ever look back from a green and think how much fun it would be to play the hole backwards? Wonder no longer. Green-to-Tee will satisfy your curiosity, though we urge you not to try this on balmy Saturday mornings.

Tee off from any convenient spot around — but never on, of course — the green and let it fly. Your target is that hole's tee. Some players play to land their balls in the tee box, while others designate a specific tee marker. Whatever, you'll find this format considerably more difficult than playing in the correct direction, simply because tee boxes are smaller than greens and few courses were built with backward play in mind. In fact, I'll go out on a limb here: **no** courses were built with backward play in mind.

Other players on the course will be fairly annoyed when you play this game. Like Cross Country, it's best tried on Tuesday evenings in the off-season. Also, this game is utterly impossible to play at Pine Valley, so don't even think about it. 🖐

Four Ball

A popular team format, Four Ball pits the best ball (net) of a team of two players against the best ball of another twosome. Each golfer plays his own ball. Use match play.

A few tips on Four Ball strategy:

- Don't get too concerned about playing (and reacting to) your opponents until late in the round. Concentrate on playing the course.

- Have the more erratic player tee off first. This lets the better golfer play it safe, if necessary.

- A player close to the hole should attempt to hole out first if he lies one more than his partner. This lets his partner putt aggressively for what may be a birdie attempt.

- Concentrate extra-hard after winning a hole. This is when most people let up.

- Never feel sorry for your opponents.

- Don't worry about how far your opponents drive the ball. Winning holes is the only thing that counts.

And some tips on selecting a partner:

- If you are a low-handicapper, pick a high one and vice versa.

- Find a consistent player relative to his handicap, often someone who's kept the same handicap for years. He usually will be the most experienced golfer in the group.

- Consider course knowledge. It matters a great deal in a match play format.

- Pick someone who is roughly the same distance off the tee. That way you can aid each other in club selection.

- Avoid hotheads or overly emotional golfers.

• Also, avoid making side bets against your partner. Concentrate on your opponents.

If one team develops such a lead that they are ahead by more holes than are left to play, that team has won. For instance, a team might be three holes up with two to play. This is called winning "three and two." At this point, players can either head to the clubhouse or play out the course for fun. Winning on the 18th hole is called winning "one up." If the match is even after 18, sudden death commences from the first tee. ▰

Long & Short

In this pair's game, the chores are divided between long shots and short shots. One player plays every shot from greater than 150 yards, and the other plays all the shorter shots. To determine team handicap, add a pair's combined handicaps and divide by three.

Long & Short amounts to an efficient division of labor, since many players with good long games have poor short games and vice versa. Partner selection requires some thought; otherwise, there's not much to recommend about this game. ▰

Vegas

Vegas is an aggressive game for foursomes. First, pair off into two teams. On each hole, take the low ball of Team A and "attach" it to the high ball. For instance, if the first player has a net three and his partner has a net five, their score for the hole is "35." Now, suppose Team B hit a net three and a net seven. Their score is "37," and they lose the hole by two points. If the stakes are a dollar a point, each player on Team B loses $2.

If a player shoots a 10 or more on a hole, the scores are automatically reversed. So, if your team has a 5 and a 10, your score is 105 — a somewhat more affordable alternative to 510.

Obviously, the key here is the low score, so avoid erratic players as partners.

And be careful about playing Vegas in the first place if you've never played before. Typically, golfers will play for a dollar a point, and the damage can really add up. In the first example, suppose the low ball on Team B was a 6 instead of a 3. Team B would lose by 32 points, or $32 each. If, for some horrible reason, both players on a team shoot double digits on the same hole, they could be out over $1,000 on one hole. Believe me, it's happened.

A Vegas variation adds a birdie incentive: If one team has one or more birdies, the score of the second team is automatically reversed. (A 46 would become a 64.) Unless you're a real thrill-seeker, Vegas is aggressive enough without this rule. Note also that Vegas tends to be on the slow side, since every golfer must finish the hole. ▪●

> "The pleasure of the long drive or the second shot to the green gives as fine an emotion as is possible for any sinner to receive on this earth."
> —R.H. Lyttleton

No Alibis

Instead of using handicaps in the normal fashion, No Alibis players may replay a certain number of shots during the round. Usually, the number of replays is three-fourths of a player's handicap. When replaying, the golfer must use the second shot, regardless of where it goes. He can't decide to play his first ball, and he can't replay the same shot twice.

No Alibis is also known as "Criers & Whiners" because it's the ideal game to play with those prone to such behavior — the sort who always follows rounds with comments like, "If I could just have that one shot back when the wind came up..." This game will shut them up. ▪●

Selected Score

In this game, each golfer plays 36 holes. Each then arrives at a final score by combining the two rounds, selecting the best net score from each of the 18 holes. The winner is the player with the lowest total.

This format is usually played with two-thirds or

three-fourths handicap.

Selected Score is a fun, leisurely format to use over a weekend, although I've seen some fanatics pack it all into one day. 🏌

Specks

Specks is a game for foursomes with, as usual, teams of two. On every hole, each team receives a "speck" for each of the following achievements:

- the longest drive on the fairway (on par-threes and -fours)

- the first ball on the green (regardless of turn and stroke number)

- the closest to the pin after everyone's on the green

- a one-putt green (up to four of these can be won)

- the low ball (net)

The team with the most specks wins either a set amount or an amount based on the speck differential. This is essentially a team version of Bingo Bango Bongo (page 19). And I don't know what a speck really is, so don't ask. 🏌

High-Low

In yet another point game for foursomes, pairs in High-Low play each hole for two points. The first point goes to the best ball; the second goes to the best of the second ball in each pair. A consistent partner is key. Play net with full handicaps. 🏌

Odd-Even

In Odd-Even, partners decide on the first tee whose score will count on the odd holes and whose will count on the evens. Use half-handicaps.

Usually, this game is a rather pointless exercise — although, as in a Scotch Foursome, there is some strategy in choosing who will drive which set of holes. 🏌

Rabbit

Rabbit is a bit like Snake (page 20), although rabbits, being cute and cuddly and all, are creatures you want to keep, not avoid.

This game works best with a threesome. When a player wins a hole (net), he takes possession of the "rabbit." The other players then try to wrest the rabbit back. To do this, any other player must beat the player holding the rabbit on any of the following holes. This then frees the rabbit to be captured by anyone, including the player who had it originally.

If the player holding the rabbit wins another hole, he then holds the rabbit, plus a "leg." This makes it harder for the others to free the rabbit, because they must first free the leg before they can free the rabbit (i.e., they must win two holes). When the rabbit is free, it's said to be "running."

The object of the game is to be in possession of the rabbit at the end of nine holes and again at the end of 18. Each of the two available rabbits is worth an agreed-upon amount. Players may also decide whether the rabbit should be set free after the front nine or carry over in someone's possession.

As well as resembling Snake, Rabbit is similar to Skins in that allegiances constantly shift. Also, strokes on late holes are critical, so avoid playing with people who get them.

I recommend playing Rabbit at the next PETA (People for the Ethical Treatment of Animals) golf outing you happen to attend. 🏌️

> **"I don't play for the scores;
> I like to play fast."**
> —**George Bush, who often plays
> 18 holes in two hours or less**

Rabbit Run

A variation of Rabbit, Rabbit Run is favored by more aggressive gamblers. In this game, a player who captures a rabbit plus a leg wins that rabbit, and he can't lose it. Another rabbit is then put into play.

If a player captures a rabbit and loses it before getting the leg, there are then two rabbits "running." Whoever wins the next hole outright then possesses the bodies of two rabbits. If he then wins another hole, he wins the two legs, and hence the permanent possession of both rabbits. If he loses the hole, the rabbits are set free — and then three rabbits are loose. Theoretically, as many as eight rabbits can be in play, so you can see how the stakes, and the pressure, can add up.

Unlike in Rabbit, the only thing in Rabbit Run that matters is who has the most complete rabbits after 18 holes. Partial possession at the end of nine or 18 doesn't count.

In a variation of this game, players must capture four legs before winning a rabbit. This isn't much fun, though, because winning four legs — when it's you against two or three others — is nearly impossible. 🍃

Worse Ball

Worse Ball is a classic sucker bet. A golfer must hit two balls on every shot and then play from the worse position, where he once again plays two balls.

Do you know an especially annoying scratch golfer? Bet him that he can't beat 45 for nine holes (or even 40 if you think he's especially stupid). Odds are very good that you'll win the bet and make the chump look foolish in the process.

Think about it. How many people make *two* good approach shots in a row? And even if they do, they'd have to sink two consecutive putts from the same spot to make birdie. In Worse Ball, birdies are virtually unknown, and pars are never plentiful. So scores are always surprisingly high.

Greg Norman probably couldn't break 40 for nine holes, so don't be shy about sticking it to your local blowhard.

A variation on this is a game called **Murphy.** Instead of using handicaps, the high-handicapper gets a certain number of "Murphies." Each Murphy lets him insist that his opponent replay a shot. As in Worse Ball, many low-handicappers underestimate how difficult this is. 🍃

Better Ball

In Better Ball, a player hits the better of two shots each time, in effect receiving a permanent mulligan. Play net with half handicaps.

Better Ball is a good confidence builder, because you'll shoot a low score and always get to correct your errors. It's a low stress game, too, unless you try to play it on a Saturday. 🍃

Backgammon

Backgammon is played between two golfers or two teams of two for a fixed amount per hole, usually a dollar. The winner of the hole wins the dollar. The twist in the game is borrowed from real backgammon, in which players may double the stakes if they think they have an advantage.

In the golf version, a player may double any time during the play of the hole, even after another player has holed out. The other player must either accept the double or decline and lose a dollar. If he accepts, the second player may then double the stakes back any time before the hole is over, and so on. (This is the same as possessing the cube in backgammon.)

Like playing with "Thirty-Two's" (see "Murphies & Garbage," page 43), doubling is often an effective way to induce a choke on the green. Play with full handicaps. 🖎

Cube

The name of Cube was borrowed from backgammon's doubling cube, and the game combines the Backgammon and Nassau formats.

Play with teams of one or two, with handicaps. The team or player with the shortest shot off the

---

Want to Feel Inadequate? Read This.

On Jan. 28, 1995, a 70-year-old golfer named Cy Young nailed two holes-in-one at the Lakeview Golf Course in Delray Beach, Florida. An extraordinary feat for anyone, of course, but it's especially amazing when you consider this fact:

Cy Young has only one arm.

On the first hole of the course, he hit a 3-iron 96 yards—and straight into the cup. He danced a little jig and continued playing the course.

On hole 13, he scored another ace, this time with a 3-wood that soared 107 yards.

As Sir Walter Simpson wrote in *The Art of Golf*, "There is no shape nor size of body, no awkwardness nor ungainliness, which puts good golf beyond reach. There are good golfers with spectacles, with one eye, with one leg, even with one arm. In golf, while there is life there is hope."

Amen.

---

first tee takes possession of the "cube," which lets his team double the units wagered on those nine holes, at their option, at any time. If they double, the cube goes to the other team, who may also double any time. Play for the 18 as well.

Cube has two optional rules, both recommended:

1. Wagers automatically double on the first hole if no one makes a net par.

2. A team making a natural birdie has the option to double before the next tee. 📖

> **"I'd rather go to the Super Bowl than shoot 70, but I'd rather shoot 65 than play in the Super Bowl."**
> **—Lawrence Taylor**

Trouble

Also known as "Disaster," Trouble is a point game in which your actual score isn't relevant, at least not directly. The goal is to collect the least number of "trouble points" possible during a round. Players shoot for a set amount per point, often a dollar. Thus, a player accumulating three trouble points owes each of his opponents three dollars.

Points are assigned as follows:

> out of bounds — 1
> water hazard — 1
> bunker — 1
> three-putt — 1
> leaving ball in bunker — 2*
> hitting from one bunker to another — 2
> four-putt — 3
> whiffed ball — 4

A player can erase all the points accumulated on a given hole by making par. At the end of the round, simply net all the points against each other and settle up.

Trouble is an excellent game for the intermediate player. Often, such players are feeling pretty smug as their handicaps drop, and they need to be taken down a notch or two. Trouble encourages smart golf (again, not to be confused with fun golf) and might just produce some surprisingly low rounds for all those would-be daredevils out there. 📖

Take an additional two points if you leave the ball in again, and so on.

Bridge

Not being much of a card player, I can only take it on faith that this game has something to do with bridge. On the other hand, I don't really care, because this is an excellent golf game for foursomes.

At the tee, one pair makes a "bid" on how many strokes (play net or gross) it will take their team to complete the hole. For instance, if they bid 10, they are betting they can play the hole in 10 strokes or fewer, combined. The bet is typically a dollar a player.

The other team then has three options:

1. Bid lower than 10.
2. Take the bet.
3. Take the bet and double it. The first team may then double it back, if they wish.

Once the bidding finishes, play the hole. One option is to add a penalty point/dollar for each stroke the winning bidder incurs over bogey. 🏌

Pig

Pig is a variation of the venerable dice game of the same name (see page 91). Each hole is worth differing amounts of points to each player. The goal is to finish the round with the greatest point total.

Here's how the points are awarded:

HOLES	NET EAGLE	NET BIRDIE	NET PAR
1–6	30 points	20 points	10 points
7–12	45 points	30 points	15 points
13–18	60 points	40 points	20 points

The catch: a net bogey means you lose all your points for that "run," which consists of as many holes as you wish.

Confused? Here's an example: Suppose a player makes par on the first three holes, thus amassing

30 points. He can then, if he wishes, announce that his run is over and he's going to bank the 30 points. Why would he do this? Because a double bogey costs all the points from a given run. This golfer doesn't want to risk losing 30 points, so he "puts them in the bank." If he banks his points, though, he must stay on the sidelines until he makes another net par. Only after this can he start another run. (Of course, he can play golf; he just can't collect any points.) Once he starts another run, he can then begin to add to his old total in the bank.

That's not quite all, though. Players scoring a quadruple bogey at any time (again, we're talking net) lose all their points from that run, as well as all their points in the bank. In other words, don't make a quadruple bogey.

After 18 holes, net out the scores. Most people play for a dime a point, and, for extra fun, add a fixed penalty, say $5, for finishing with no points. Watch out for those quadruple bogeys on 18!

Bobby Jones

In Bobby Jones's famous series of instructional videos, there's a wonderful segment where some long-forgotten actor challenges Jones to play the Riviera Golf Club even-up. The catch? Jones must play the actor's tee shots and vice versa. The twist was designed to put Jones in some difficult situations that, needless to say, he rises above to make his opponent's billfold lighter.

Try playing Bobby Jones when matched against someone of a vastly different handicap (assuming you trust your opponent to hit his best tee shots). Be sure to play the back tees to make it as interesting as possible. ▣●

Chairman

In Chairman, a game for threesomes only, the first player to win a hole outright becomes the "chairman" and assumes the chair. Each hole that a player wins outright while occupying the chair is worth one unit each from the other players. Play with full handicap.

If the chairman ties another player, he doesn't win a unit, but he retains the chair. The chair passes, although no units are awarded, when another player wins a hole outright. That player must then win an additional hole to win any units.

Basically, it's a variation of Rabbit. ▣●

English

Here's another point game for threesomes only. In English, players can get six points on each hole in one of four ways, depending on the distribution of scores:

1. a. Player with lowest score: 4 points
   b. Player with next-to-lowest score: 2 points
   c. Last player: 0 points

2. a. Two players with lowest scores: 3 points
   b. Last player: 0 points

3. a. Player with lowest score: 4 points
   b. Two other players tied: 1 point each

4. a. Three players tied: 2 points each

The simple way to play this is "most points wins." Alternatively, each player can play a Nassau, using points instead of holes, versus each of the others. Or, a third option is to net points against each other at the end. 🏌

GolFact

At the 1935 Masters, Gene Sarazen sunk a four-wood brassie for a double-eagle on the 15th hole. Over the years, according to Sarazen, probably 20,000 people claimed to have witnessed the event. In reality, only about 15 people were there, and three of them were Bobby Jones, Walter Hagen, and Sarazen himself—the three greatest golfers of the day. Apparently, Hagen was happy about the shot because he was late for a date.

Nine Point

Nine Point is similar to English but played with foursomes. Points are awarded per hole as follows:

a. Player with lowest score: 5 points
b. Next-to-lowest score: 3 points
c. Third-lowest score: 1 point
d. Lowest score: 0 points

In case of ties, divide the points up, as in English. Two players who tie for first, for instance, would each get four points ($\{5+3\}/2$).

Myself, I don't much like Nine Point or English. There's really no strategy except "play golf as well as you can." 🏌

Bogey Man

In Bogey Man, the first player to make a net bogey owes each of the other players one unit, and he must continue paying one unit per hole until someone else bogeys. The new Bogey Man continues in the same fashion.

Aggressive gamblers will want to add a unit for

each hole. (In other words, on your second hole as the Bogey Man you owe two additional units, on the third hole three units, etc.)

If you prefer, use double bogeys instead. ▰

Chug 'n Chop

In this game, a player (using one-quarter handicap) who wins a hole must chug a beer before the next tee. Otherwise, play a standard Nassau.

Another way to play is with shots of whiskey or tequila, in which case the game is called "Shots."

Use the minimal handicaps, because better players will find their games diminished by the bottle as soon as they win a hole or two. And if you want to steer clear of the county lock-up, make the drinks on the small side. No Foster's "oil cans" here, please.

I recommend Chug 'n Chop for play at municipal links or at exclusive private clubs — where you aren't a member. ▰

> **"The most exquisitely satisfying act in the world of golf is that of throwing a club. The full backswing, the delayed wrist action, the flowing follow-through, followed by that unique whirring sound, reminiscent only of a passing flock of starlings, are without parallel in sport."**
>
> **—Henry Longhurst**

Club & Ball Verities

Ever notice how every club has at least one guy who claims to know everything about club design? Ever notice how this person gets on your nerves? Well, the next time he corners you with gratuitous advice on hosels and hookspin, arm yourself. Here are a few myth-busting items, compiled from research done by Bob McClure and the USGA, that will put that tedious know-it-all in his place:

❏ Ever encounter a "persimmon snob?" You know the type: he uses only a persimmon driver, eschewing modern technology, because the "feel" is so superior. In fact, "laminated rock maple woods," i.e. regular old woods, are superior in every respect to persimmon. They are stronger and therefore more resistant to cracking, chipping, and warping. No one can feel the difference between laminated maple and persimmon, no matter what Nicklaus thinks. Furthermore, laminated club heads have a constant density, something not always true of persimmon. This means that, if anything, the "feel" of laminated club heads should be better.

❏ There is no difference in the feel between forged and cast irons.

❏ Graphite shafts produce only two to three yards more distance versus steel shafts, assuming all other variables are constant.

❏ *What about ball design know-it-alls?* you ask. What about the 20-handicapper who will use only Titleist balatas? Here's a zinger for them: It has been conclusively proven (by obscuring ball identity to a group of test golfers) that there is no difference in the "feel" between surlyn and balata covered balls. None could tell the difference when they didn't know what they were hitting. The main difference is that balata balls will spin more, giving exceptional golfers the ability to "shape" shots. For the rest of us, though, balatas will only turn fades into slices. In other words, unless you're a damn good golfer, they are actually worse for your game.

CHAPTER 2

Murphies & Garbage: Optional Rules & Side Bets

Murphies

Murphy: A player off the green (as well as off the fringe) may declare a "Murphy," whereby he must get up-and-down to win units from each of the other players.

Overs: Whenever a player whines about his luck—or just complains about his shot—before the ball comes to rest, he can be forced to hit again if another player declares "Overs." This is especially handy for use against the type of golfer who shoots a 79 and still says he was robbed.

Scruffy: A player hitting an awful tee shot may call a "Scruffy," which lets him bet a unit against all the other players that he can make par (gross). The other players must agree to the bet. A player may call a Scruffy after a good tee shot as well. If it's a difficult hole, his opponents might still be wise to take the bet.

Thirty-Two's: This is a "call" bet invoked when a player thinks his opponent on the green will three-putt. The challenger must give 3:2 odds. The other

player may decline. It can be quite effective to offer Thirty-Two's at a crucial juncture in a match—even if your opponent doesn't have a difficult putt—because it's really unnerving to some players. You may lose the side bet, but it might help you win the match.

Fort Worth Rules: If a player—a male player—fails to hit past the women's tee on his tee shot, he must finish the hole with his, er, "niblick" hanging out of his trousers. Those who find it necessary may remove their spikes. Also known as "Tennessee Rules."

Total Putts: The player with the fewest putts over a round or tournament wins. First cut of fringe counts. This is a helpful format to add to matches, because it keeps players interested until the end, even if they're out of the match. ♣

Garbage

"Garbage" is the common term to describe a collection of side bets popular with golfers otherwise playing, for example, Skins or a Nassau. You probably know about "Greenies," "Sandies," and "Birdies," but have you heard of "Watsons?" How about "Froggies?" Winning a garbage bet is usually worth one point (usually a dollar) each from the other players or team.

Some advice: Don't play too many garbage bets at once, because the confusion can detract from your enjoyment of the game. And note that, unlike the other side bets and rules that follow, garbage bets are agreed upon at the beginning of a round. Also, no handicap strokes are allowed.

Arnies: won by scoring par and never once touching the fairway. Also called "Seves."

Bambis: scoring par after striking a live animal.

Barfies: won by throwing up at any time during a hole and still scoring par. (It's been done, trust me.) Applies equally to hangovers, food poisoning, and chemotherapy reactions. Also called "Buicks" and "Fairway Pizzas."

Barkies: hitting a tree and still making par. Leaves don't count; everyone must hear good, solid wood. The rare "Double Barkie," worth two points, involves hitting two trees and still making par. Also called "Woodies" and "Seves."

Birdies: scoring a birdie or better.

Carpets: winning a Greenie (see below) on every par-three. This doubles the payout on the Greenies.

Chippies: making an up-and-down from anywhere around the green (not including the fringe).

Flaggies: hitting your tee shot on any hole to within a flag stick's distance of the cup.

Froggies: successfully skipping a shot across a water hazard.

Greenies: being the closest to the pin on a par-three. Player must one- or two-putt to win. If no one hits the green, no one wins. Carryovers are optional.

Goosies: tagging a goose with a golf club; worth one unit. (See also page 78)

Hogans: playing a hole in regulation while never having your ball out of the fairway. The guys I play with tend to make more Bambis.

Moles: Roughly the opposite of a Sandie (below); golfers pay their opponents one unit for each sand shot left in a bunker.

Municipals: making par on a hole while playing an adjoining fairway.

Nicklauses: striking the longest drive that remains in the fairway on each par-four or -five.

Ouzle-Fouzle: An Ouzle is the Scottish term for a Greenie. A Fouzle is what happens if you win an Ouzle and then three-putt. In Greenies, a player simply forfeits his winnings, but with a Fouzle, he must pay each of the other players one unit.

Polies: One unit is earned for each putt sunk from outside the length of the flag stick.

Sandies: getting up-and-down from a bunker. Fairway bunkers are included.

Splashies: making par after hitting into the water (whether the ball was lost or not); can be combined with Froggies.

Super Sandies: making par or better from a fairway bunker.

Watsons: chipping into a hole from off the green, regardless of score.

"He's long, the Lama."

Who hit the longest drive ever? The longest drive ever in a P.G.A. event was a 412-yard shot in 1990 by — well, who cares, because we're just getting warmed up here. The longest drive in the history of major championships was a 430-yard blast by Craig Wood on the fifth hole at St. Andrews during the 1933 British Open. Good, but not good enough.

The longest drive ever hit in competition was 515 yards by 64-year-old Mike Austin at the National Seniors Open in 1974. With a 35 m.p.h. tailwind at the Winterwood Golf Club in Las Vegas, he drove the ball 65 yards *past* the green on a 450-yard par four.

But who said this had to be *real* golf?

Many golfers believe that Alan Shepard struck the longest ball ever, on the moon in 1971, during the Apollo 14 mission. Certainly Shepard *thought* he was going into the record books.

After hitting in front of millions of TV viewers, Shepard, a 12-handicap from Texas, reported to Mission Control that the ball "went for miles and miles." Well, that was golfer hyperbole at its best. Using a makeshift six-iron, Shepard shanked his first shot into a crater 40 yards away. His second shot traveled about 200 yards — not too impressive when you consider that the moon's gravity is one-sixth that of earth's, but not bad for a guy wearing huge gloves, oxygen tanks, and a pressurized space suit. And despite the potentially huge endorsement money, Shepard has never revealed the golf ball brand.

So maybe Arnold Palmer holds the record since, in 1976, he hit a drive off the Eiffel Tower? Nope, not even close.

Perhaps the irrepressible Irish club pro Liam Higgins from Waterville thought he, too, was going to break a record when he teed one up on an airport runway in Dublin in 1984, but the ball went a wee 634 yards. In the category of runway golf, John Daly later hit one 880 yards down a runway in mile-high Denver. But neither was the longest ever.

The real winner of the all-time "Big Shillelagh Award," on this or any other celestial body, is an Australian meteorologist named Nils Lied. In 1962, Nils teed up a bright orange ball on a glacier in Antarctica and poked it a smooth 1.5 miles. (He did, in fact, find the ball to confirm the distance.)

> **"When I look on my life and try to decide out of what have I got the most actual pleasure, I have no doubt at all in saying that I have got more out of golf than anything else."**
>
> — Lord Barbazon, *The Barbazon Story*

CHAPTER 3

Tournament Formats

Medal Play

Also known as Stroke Play, Medal Play is the most basic format for golf tournaments. Contestants simply play 18 holes, and prizes go to players with the best gross scores and net scores. Use handicaps from 80-100% — preferably on the lower side to prevent sandbagging.*

Medal Play is the most serious and least forgiving tournament format (no gimmies!), so it's often used for club championships. ▪●

Sandbagging: when a player wins a match or tournament because of an inappropriately high handicap. Handicap committees should prevent such situations, but often can't — or don't care to — police thoroughly.

Match Play against Par

The format here is match play, but rather than playing another golfer, your opponent is "Old Man Par" himself. If you make a net birdie, you go "one up." If you make a net bogey, you are "one down," and so on. The winner is the most up against par.

If you find yourself in trouble, take risks, because a triple-bogey is no worse than a bogey in this format. And take advantage of stroke holes. ▪●

The Calloway System

The Calloway System is an excellent choice for company outings and the like, where accurate handicaps are difficult to gauge—and some participants may not even *have* a handicap. The aim is to compare "core" scores of all players, regardless of talent.

The net score of each player is determined by making an adjustment, based on discarded holes, to the gross score. The higher the gross score, the greater the adjustment. For instance, someone shooting 90 may deduct his two worst holes. If he shot seven on both holes, his net score becomes 76 (90 minus 14).

Consult the following table for adjustments:

If your score is	*Deduct*
less than 73	0 holes
73-75	half of worst hole
76-80	worst hole
81-85	1.5 worst holes
86-90	2 worst holes
91-95	2.5 worst holes
96-100	3 worst holes
101-105	3.5 worst holes
106-110	4 worst holes
And so on...	

Half-strokes get rounded up. Though somewhat arbitrary, the Calloway System rewards golfers who play consistently but suffer a brief lapse or two.

An optional rule that makes good sense: don't allow any deductions of the 17th or 18th holes. Players should always feel the pressure down the stretch. ▰

The Peoria System

Like the Calloway System, the Peoria System is employed in a tournament when, for whatever reason, handicaps can't be.

After all players have teed off, select six holes (preferably two par-threes, two par-fours, and two par-fives). After players finish, total each player's score on the selected holes, multiply by three, and subtract par for the course. This determines that player's Peoria handicap for the day. Subtract that amount from the player's gross score to determine his net result.

For example, say a player shot 32 on the six selected holes; 32 times 3 equals 96. Assuming a course par of 72, 96 minus 72 equals 24. If the player shot 93 for the day, his final net score would be 69 (93 minus 24). 🖊

The Stableford System

The Stableford System of scoring, also known as "The Good, the Bad, and the Ugly," has grown in stature since the start of the International, an annual tournament at Castle Pines in Colorado. Popular in Britain for some time, the Stableford is an exciting format to watch because it favors risk-taking.

The system is a point game in which points are awarded as follows:

Eagle — 4 points
Birdie — 3 points
Par — 2 points
Bogey — 1 point
Double Bogey or worse — 0 points

In each case, it's the net score that counts. The winner is the player with the highest point total.

As I've said, smart golf and fun golf are often mutually exclusive. It's certainly fun to go for a 500-yard par-five over water in two strokes, but it isn't smart. Stableford, because it rewards such risks, makes fun golf and smart golf the same thing. I highly recommended this system for players and spectators alike.

Note: Since no points are awarded for scores worse than bogey, players should pick-up when appropriate. 🖊

The Chapman System (a.k.a. Pinehurst)

The Chapman System, sometimes called "The Pinehurst System," is often used for mixed-sex events. Teams are generally mixed pairs, and each player hits a drive and then plays his/her partner's second shot. From there, the team decides which ball is better to play. On par-three's, the team must choose after the tee shot. They then play that ball out by alternating shots. Usually, it's best to use 75% of average handicap.

Since more and more women are taking up golf each year, the Chapman System is increasingly popular. ▣●

Tournament Nassau

The Nassau format, used primarily in foursomes, can be modified for use in tournaments. Teams, which can consist of individuals, twosomes, or foursomes, simply take strokes on the holes where they apply, and prizes are awarded for the best front nine, the best back nine, and the best 18. (In the case of teams, take the best ball on each hole.)

Nassau Tournaments are similar to Medal Play with handicap (page 50), except not as severe. Players starting poorly, for instance, can still recover and win a prize. ▣●

One-Club

This is as simple as it sounds. One-Club makes golfers play an entire tournament (generally one round only—this is a novelty format, after all)

with only one club. Two-, Three-, and Four-Club tournaments are also popular.

Obviously, club selection is the paramount issue. In fact, it's the only issue. Since versatility is the key, most players immediately rule out their woods and high irons. The five-iron seems to be the preferred stick by most One-Club contestants, although I'm partial to a six or seven.

Though the One-Club format seems gimmicky, it tends to reward intelligent, creative golfers. A wide variety of shots are called for, and players will learn some useful skills, such as how to add and subtract loft from their shots.

How well can someone play golf with one club? Pretty well, if you ask Thad Daber. He shot a 70 using only his six-iron at the 1987 World One-Club Championship at the par-72 Lochmere Golf Club in Cary, North Carolina. ▣●

> **"Unlike the other Scotch game of whisky drinking, excess in golf is not injurious to the health." —Sir Walter Simpson**

No-Club

Yes, some people have even played tournaments with no clubs. The general idea is to throw your way around the course. Unless you've been playing a lot of baseball lately, this format falls in the "Do not try this at home—or sober" category. You'll throw out your arm after two or three tosses, and if you continue playing, you'll suffer enormous pain in your triceps the next day.

Nevertheless, a college student named Joe Flynn (on the school's baseball team, one presumes) once "threw" a round of 82 at the Port Royal Golf Club in Bermuda. Apparently, a No-Club Tournament was part of the Spring Break festivities there in 1975. Flynn, besides having a rubber arm, devised an interesting technique for putts inside eight feet: He would hold the ball over his head and fall flat on his face. An instant before facial impact, Flynn would dunk the ball into the hole. Consult a physician before trying this one.

For his efforts, Flynn received a case of beer and a place, however minute, in golf history.

Scramble

In a Scramble, each foursome is a team competing against all other foursomes. Each player in the group drives off the tee, then all four golfers play their second shots from the best-driven ball. All then play their third shots from the best second ball, and so on. Each player in a foursome must have at least four of their drives used by the group. Don't wait until the end!

Handicaps are not used during play, but they are used to create teams. All players should split into four handicap groups (lowest to highest). Use four hats, and pick a player from each hat to form a team. "A" and "B" players should tee off from the back markers.

A Scramble usually calls for a shotgun start, preceded by lunch or followed by dinner. Seven- or eight-under is usually the score to beat. 🏌

Honesty

Prior to teeing off, each Honesty participant (anywhere from a twosome to an entire tournament) predicts their gross score on a piece of paper and antes a given amount. Whoever hits the score on the nose, or whoever is closest, wins the pot. Ties are split accordingly.

Players getting more than a double bogey on holes 17 or 18 are automatically eliminated. This prevents players from padding their scores to win the tournament.

Honesty can be a fun side bet to your normal game. 🏌

Get Odds Next Time, Wally

Amazing everyone but himself, Walter Hagen once made a $10 bet that he would make a hole-in-one — and then proceeded to knock the ball right into the hole. "The trick is to know when it's about to happen," he explained.

String

An interesting game, String lets players decide over the course of a round how and when to improve their lies.

Each player needs a length of string and a pair of scissors or a knife. You can use your string at any time to improve the position of your ball. But use it sparingly! Each time you use it, you must cut off and discard the amount of string used.

For instance, suppose on the first fairway your ball lands in a nasty divot. If you could just move your ball three inches, you'd have a great lie. So, use three inches of string and move your ball safely out of the hole. But you must cut off and discard three inches of string, leaving you less string for future use.

You may move the ball in any direction, including forward. You can even use string to sink a putt, but since this maneuver costs a stroke, it's a fairly dumb idea. Some good places to use your string are buried bunker lies, heavy greenside rough, swing-obstructed lies, and so forth.

You can't use string for relief from a hazard if you can't find the ball in the first place. Just because you saw your ball go into the pond six inches from the edge doesn't mean you can put a new ball in play without penalty. If you can find your ball, though, you can use string to gain relief from a hazard.

The Tournament Committee should decide the length of string for each player. String can even be used as a handicap in lieu of, or in addition to, strokes. Give the high handicappers an extra foot, for instance. Or award one foot per handicap stroke. Be judicious, though. Clever players can save nearly a stroke for every three or four inches of string. And high handicappers will also have more opportunities to put the string to use, getting more efficient use per inch. ▣

Chicago

Chicago is essentially a creative handicapping method. Players receive a negative quota of points, called a "hurdle," based on their handicaps. Scratch players get -39 points, one-handicaps get -38, two-handicaps get -37, and so on to 36-handicaps, who get -3.

> **"Can you name me a single case where devotion to this pestilential pastime has done a man any practical good?"**
> **—P.G. Wodehouse,**
> **The Clicking of Cuthbert**

Then, based on their performances, players receive positive points as follows:

Bogeys = 1 point
Pars = 2 points
Birdies = 4 points
Eagles = 8 points

The player who clears his "hurdle" by the most points wins. If no one clears, the player closest to zero wins. Wagering can involve a fixed sum to the winner or an amount based on point differentials. You can also add a bonus for anyone clearing his hurdle. ▣

Field Day

Field Day is a straightforward, one-day, member/guest tournament format in which club members are required to invite three guests each, thus creating foursomes. Teams match their best ball of four against other teams' best to determine the winners. Prizes are awarded for best ball gross and best ball net (often 12- or 13-under). Generally, clubs will offer numerous side prizes as well: longest drive, closest to the pin, best guest score, etc.

Field Day should always climax with a boisterous dinner and awards ceremony. It's an excellent format for scouting potential club members in a relaxed environment. 🔲

Shoot-Out

To play Shoot-Out, assemble 19 players at the first tee. All 19, as a single group, play the first hole. Whoever has the highest net ball on the hole can hit the showers. If there's a tie, the players involved engage in a "chip-off," whereby everyone chips from the same spot. The spot is chosen by a non-participant before the round and marked with chalk. (The spot can also be on the green, as long as it creates a ridiculously long putt.) The golfer farthest from the hole after the chip or putt is then eliminated. Shoot-Out places a heavy emphasis on the short game.

The remaining 18 players move to the second hole, where they hit in reverse order, since teeing-off late is strategically helpful. This is not a game for risk-taking unless you know you must.

Play continues with one golfer losing on each hole until a victor emerges at #18.

Because Shoot-Out is extremely slow and can tie up a course for hours, many clubs opt for a ten-player, nine-hole format, popularized by the annual Merrill Lynch Pro Shoot-Out. Teams of two, alternating shots, works also. 🔲

Get-Acquainted Tournament

Typically played at the beginning of the season, a Get-Acquainted Tournament is usually one round of golf and can have any format that utilizes pairs. The catch: you must select a partner with whom you have never played. Since some people are a little shy about this, it helps to have the tournament organizer act as a catalyst, perhaps suggesting pairings or drawing names from a hat.

Consolation Tournament

Also called "Last Chance," this is a tournament for the end of the season, after all other tournaments have been played. Players can use any format. The only catch: the field is open only to golfers who haven't won any tournament prizes during the year. Keep a low profile.

Drop-Out

A combination of Match Play against Par and Shoot-Out, Drop-Out requires match play against par (using strokes) on each hole, but players must quit as soon as they lose a hole. The

winner is whoever makes it farthest around the course.

Drop-Out is basically pretty pointless. I prefer one format or the other. ♨

Flag Tournament

In a Flag Tournament, each player receives a certain number of strokes — usually the course par plus two-thirds of the player's full handicap. So, a 15-handicapper on a par-72 course gets 82 strokes. He then plays 82 shots and stops, planting a flag on the spot where his 82nd shot lands.

The flags should be provided on the first tee by the tournament director. Each participant should have his name taped to his flag. This way, as players make their way through the back nine, they can see where others bit the dust.

If a player finishes all 18 holes before using his total strokes, he should either keep playing until he's out of strokes or stop. Under the first option, the winner is the player who plants his flag farthest on the course. Under the second, the winner is whoever has the most strokes remaining after 18 holes. The reason two-thirds handicap is used, though, is so most people will finish somewhere inside of regulation.

One additional rule: You can't plant a flag past a hole that you haven't completed. In other words, if you're five feet short of a green with one stroke left, you can't blast the ball with your 2-iron onto the next fairway. Also, if the farthest two players both finish on the same green, the winner is the golfer closer to the hole.

A Flag Tournament is essentially Stroke Play with handicap, but the twist makes it a little more interesting.

The USGA notes, appropriately, that American flags should never be used as markers. ♨

GolFact

No one has ever sunk a putt greater than four feet to win the U.S. Open, knowing that he had to make the putt.

Kicker's Tournament

In this format, the tournament committee picks a number at random, usually between 60 and the course par. This number remains a secret until the end of the tournament. Players then select whatever handicap they want. The object is to end up with a net score that's as close as possible to the secret number. The player whose score is closest to, or equals, the secret number is the winner.

A Kicker's Tournament is rare, and for good reason: It's utterly pointless. You might as well just have a lottery on the first tee and be done with it. The only situation in which I can imagine using this format is if you're playing with strangers you don't trust. Even then, the Chapman System (page 52) is preferable. ▣

Throw-Out

In a Throw-Out tournament, golfers play 18 holes of Medal Play with handicap and, at the conclu-sion, delete their scores on a specific number of holes (usually three). The winner is the golfer with the lowest net on the remaining holes.

Handicaps should not be played at 100%. Try reducing them in proportion with the hole reduction. So, for instance, if you're using 15 holes, set handicaps at 15/18th's, or 83%, rounded to the nearest whole number. ▣

Fewest Putts

Okay, folks, don't shoot the messenger on this one. In this format, the player who hits the fewest putts wins. Period. Only strokes on the green count (i.e., the fringe doesn't), and no handicaps are used.

When I first heard about this game, I was a little perplexed. Do people really play it? The ideal strategy makes for some lame golf: Players should hit to the exact spot on the green, no matter how many shots it takes, that gives them the easiest approach to the pin. That's not only stupid, it's also painfully slow.

However, you can make this a much better game by adjusting the putting total by each player's net score. That way, people won't play like wimps. For instance, you could establish a scale like this:

If you shoot a net	*Add this many strokes*
under 66	0
66-70	2
71-75	4
76-80	6
81-85	8
And so on... 🏌️	

Blind Holes

Blind Holes blends skill and luck. The winner is selected based on his score for nine holes that are chosen at random by the pro or tournament chairman after golfers have teed off. Use Medal Play

and half-handicaps. Basically, this is a twist on Throw-Out and not particularly interesting. 🏌️

Three's, Four's, & Five's

In this format, prizes go to the players scoring, separately, the most three's, four's, and five's on a net basis, using full handicaps.

The main thing that makes this game interesting is that players must decide after 12 or 13 holes which prize to play for, although intentionally blowing putts to make a four or five is considered pretty cheesy. 🏌️

Sixes

In Sixes, foursomes play as a team for gross and net prizes. For the first six holes, use the best ball. For the middle six, use the two best balls. For the final six, use three and then add up the totals. Pressure builds, as it should, toward the end. 🏌️

Bong

No, this tournament does not involve a long plastic pipe filled with a substance that a certain U.S. President never inhaled. The main idea in Bong is simple: avoid mistakes. In this game, golfers get points for a variety of sins. The player with the fewest points wins.

One caveat: To win, a player must shoot a gross score within five strokes of his handicap. This prevents weasels from putting their way around the golf course.

Error	Points
three-putt	2
four-putt	3
lost ball	2
out-of-bounds	2
hit into sand	1
hit into water	1
ball left in trap	3
hit one trap to another	2
whiff	4

Bong is an excellent format for golfers who need to develop a sense of course management. It can also be used for intra-foursome games. 🏌

Nutshell Tournament

Nutshell is a good format for company outings and the like, where time is limited and you want people to mingle. After players qualify in the early morning (using full handicaps) over nine holes, place qualifiers into flights of eight. The top qualifier for each flight meets the lowest qualifier, #2 meets #7, etc. Entrants then play Match Play over nine holes using 80% of their handicaps.

It will take three matches of nine holes to determine each flight's winner. If things are run efficiently, the whole tournament can be accomplished in one day. Follow up with cocktails and an awards dinner. On the whole, a Nutshell Tournament makes for a really fun day. 🏌

Monster Day

Put the tees and pins in the most ridiculous, insane places possible. Place the tees all the way back. Put them five feet apart at an angle. Whatever. Then find the hardest pin positions on every green, even if

they're illegal. (Normally, a pin must be a certain distance from the fringe and can't be on too much of a slope.) Then, most important, have fun and don't whine.

Another option: Put in two-pin placements on each green, both in ridiculous positions. Players hit for whichever they think is easier, which will really add some strategy to the round.

Monster Day is also known as "Ball Buster."

Pink Ball

To play Pink Ball, use teams of four. Each foursome has a hideous, bright pink ball that rotates among players. (Of course, the ball can be any color, but the more obnoxious, the better.) Player 1 uses it on the first hole, player 2 on the second, and so on. Take the best two net scores on each hole and add them. Whoever has the pink ball on a given hole must contribute one of the two scores.

> **"The Lord answers my prayers everywhere except on the course."**
> — **Rev. Billy Graham**

One variation: The golfer with the pink ball is automatically disqualified if he loses it. This is perhaps too harsh, so I don't recommend it. Players should have a reason to stay interested, after all.

Another, less harsh, variation: Keep the overall net score for the pink ball separately, and give a prize to the team with the best pink ball score. If a team loses the pink ball, it's out. This makes for considerable camaraderie (and tension) if you're playing on a course with a lot of water. ✒●

Monkey Tournament

A Monkey Tournament, played with teams of four or even five, begins by placing the name of each club from a full bag in a hat. Each player from each team then selects a club from the hat, and that's the only club he can use for the entire round.

The players on each team alternate shots for 18 holes. When it's your turn to hit, you must use your chosen club, regardless of the situation. Half of average team handicap is suggested.

This format is good for lots of yucks and stories at the 19th hole afterwards. Imagine hitting drivers out of pot bunkers or teeing off with a sand wedge. Also, despite high scoring, it's a fairly quick format, so it's good for the afternoon round of a 36-hole outing. ✒●

Beer Golf

I played golf exactly twice in college, sort of. My fraternity had an annual spring outing to the Yale Golf Course where, like every other conceivable activity, we found it necessary to add beer to the proceedings.

The rules, if not the results, were very straightforward. Players could deduct one stroke from their scores for every beer they consumed over 13 holes. I don't remember why we played exactly 13 holes, but it had always been that way, and you don't mess with tradition in a fraternity. I suspect it had something to do with getting back to campus in time for dinner. Or happy hour.

The winner was the player with the lowest net: strokes minus beers consumed. Handicaps are not used. In our case, they were irrelevant since we all would have been about a 40.

Many beer golfers use the strategy of trying to down about one beer per hole and then chugging as many as possible on the last fairway. Those choosing a more ambitious pace discover the Law of Diminishing Returns. Many also discover the meaning of "octuple bogey."

In order to keep everyone supplied with beer, someone should drive a fully stocked cart around constantly. (I am somewhat, although not entirely, embarrassed to say that we called this person the "cart wench.")

Beer Golf is usually played as a fraternity or club outing, which highlights some of the game's disadvantages. First, players must actually plan ahead, a concept foreign to the sort of people inclined to play Beer Golf in the first place.

Second, Beer Golf can rarely be played twice on the same course—with management's permission, that is. It seems that greens keepers are not amused by carts floating in water hazards, pins being tossed like javelins, etc. (The greens keeper at Yale was a uniquely understanding fellow.)

Incidentally, there's even a variation of this game: drink before the match and adjust handicaps by one for each beer or drink consumed. So, a player with four handicap who tosses back a six-pack can play with a ten. You can also add penalties and side bets for players who need bathroom breaks, players who hurl, etc., but this is getting out of hand, so let's move on… ▇●

Miscellaneous Records, Continued

Longest double-eagle on record: 647 yards by naval officer Kevin Murray at the Guam Navy Golf Club in 1982 (2nd hole).

Fewest putts in 18 holes: 15. This feat has been accomplished by two men, Richard Stanwood in 1976 and Ed Drysdale in 1985.

Most courses played: Ralph Kennedy of New York City has reportedly played 3,625 different courses. If you played a new course every day, it would take you ten years to top this mark.

CHAPTER 4

Gambling Tournaments

Blind Partners

In this format, each player antes $50 (to be award-ed later to the winning team) in a pot prior to the round. Players then tee off with anyone they choose in a shotgun start, using stroke play with an 80-90% handicap. During dinner, partners are drawn at random. Note that partners are drawn only *after* play is completed. The winner is the "team" (twosomes or foursomes) with the lowest total score. Pretty simple, pretty dull.

To make this more interesting, try "continuous betting" on the outcome. It works as follows: Initially, each player "owns" himself, so if he and his to-be-named partner win the tournament, they split the pot. But in a "continuous betting" format, a player may sell the rights to himself any time before the winning team is determined (i.e., after all the partners are selected).

So, you can sell yourself before you start, dur-ing the round, after the round, during the picking of partners, whenever. You can even sell yourself after your partner has been selected, assuming all the partners have not yet been drawn. If you're matched early with someone who shot a low score, your value should skyrocket.

Further, whoever buys your rights may turn around and sell those rights to someone else.

Players can be "shorted," as well. This means you can sell a player you don't even own. The risk is that you must match half the pot as payment to the buyer if the player actually wins. (One way to avoid this is to "cover" your short, which means you buy the rights to the player from someone else. If the market value of the player has declined in the interim, you've made a profit, as well having convinced everyone what a brilliant, stud-horse trader you are.)

Needless to say, dinner can become a frenzy of speculative fever. This is good. In fact, it's the point. Blind Partners is pretty dull without gambling.

A variation: Tee off in the morning, choose partners at lunch, and then schedule a second round that golfers must play with their drawn partner. Again, buying and selling can occur anytime until the end of the tournament. 🏌

GolFact

The longest hole-in-one ever recorded was on a 444-yard hole. Bob Mitera made the ace at the aptly-named Miracle Hill Country Club in Omaha, Nebraska in 1965. Bob had a major tailwind, and the hole is downhill.

Calcutta

A Calcutta is not a tournament format so much as a gambling format for Match Play tournaments using the "four ball" format. Teams, usually twosomes, first qualify for different "flights." A flight is a draw of eight or 16 teams. The top qualifying teams are placed in the Championship flight, the next group in the First flight, the next in the Second, and so on.

The qualifying round is often played on Friday and followed by the Calcutta Dinner on Friday evening—which can be the ultimate exercise in male bonding. Allow me to set the stage: lots of men in blue blazers, much beer and brandy, cigars everywhere. Bawdy stories and whopping lies are mandatory. Dinner should involve red meat of some kind and should be followed by a highly caloric dessert.

Over a good port and cigars, the Calcutta, or auction, begins. The auctioneer — try for someone with an outgoing personality who's familiar with most of the participants — must both oversee the bidding process and dole out heaps of good-natured abuse to anyone and everyone.

The auction process is simple: teams are sold to the highest bidder. Whoever owns the winning team in a flight collects 70% of that flight's pot, and the owner of the runner-up team collects 30%. The members of a given team, if they don't actually purchase themselves, may buy half of their team from the team owner for a specified amount, say $250, or one-half the purchase price, whichever is less.

Tournament officials must put some thought into setting the "insider's" price, because it affects the overall level of bidding. The lower the price, the lower the bidding. The insider price is used by most clubs as a way to keep the pot at levels that won't attract the attention of local authorities or cause members to sue each other later.

Incidentally, it's considered good sportsmanship to buy half of your own team, thus expressing your commitment to your "owner." Also, it's typical to auction only the top two or three flights due to time and alcohol considerations. ≡●

Win, Place, & Show

Also known as a "Pari-mutuel," Win, Place, & Show usually involves a pre-tournament betting dinner similar to a Calcutta. The difference is that the betting is on foursomes, and the payoff is patterned after horse racing.

Teams can either sign up in advance or be drawn out of a hat at the dinner. Once the teams are established, however, there is no general auction as in a Calcutta. This is because you may not want other people to know how you're betting.

Bettors approach the event organizer, usually the club pro, and wager in $5 increments on teams to win, place, or show (finish first, second, or third). If you bet "one unit on team 6 to place," you're betting $5 on team 6 to finish first or second. Bets can be accepted until the last foursome has left the tee.

Team scores are determined by adding the two best balls (net) on each hole. Play with full handicaps.

Once play has ended, divide the pool into 40 parts and split it as follows:

	Win	Place	Show
winning foursome	16 parts	8 parts	4 parts
second place		6 parts	3 parts
third place			3 parts

All bettors on the winning team share the win-money, which is 16/40th's (or 40%, for those of you who passed seventh grade) of the total pool. So, for example, if the total pool was $500, and if ten people had bet one unit each on the winning team, the team members would each receive $50. If five people bet one unit and one person bet five units, the five gets $50 and the person betting five units wins $250.

A strategy tip: Make bets that others are avoiding. That way, should you win, you don't have to divide your share into as many pieces. Also, don't bet more than one unit on any team, as it is of little incremental value.

Sweeps Tournament

This is an interesting version of the Calcutta. Like the Calcutta, there should be a dinner with lots of booze, cigars, and good-natured ribbing. However, bidding is based on handicaps, not dollars. And use stroke play instead of match. Each team of two sells for the same amount, usually $100.

Here's how it works: Suppose the combined handicap of the first team at auction is 25. The bidding should start at 30, or a five-stroke discount. Thus, if you buy the team at 30, you get its combined gross better-ball score plus 30. (A team selling at a five-stroke discount isn't getting much respect.)

The bidding then progresses to lower numbers

> **"My favorite shots are the practice swing and the conceded putt. The rest can never be mastered."**
> **—Lord Robertson**

until someone owns the team. In the example above, a bid of 25 would be "par," and anything lower would be deemed a "premium."

The winner of the "sweeps" pool is the owner of the team with the lowest adjusted score over the number of rounds played (usually two). Note that since the adjusted score is not the same as each team's handicaps, the winners of the "official" tournament and the "sweeps" tournament are often not the same.

Each team may buy a 25% interest in itself for 25% of the fixed auction price. And be sure to give some of the pot to second and third place, plus offer some daily prizes.

A Sweeps auction can be bruising for a golfer's ego when he goes for a discount. And, while golfers trading for significant premiums might feel pretty good about themselves, on another day they'd be derided as "sandbaggers." ▐●

Tour Quiz

Q: What is the difference in scoring average between the best tour players and the worst?
A: About two strokes.

Q: What is the longest course on the tour?
A: Castle Pines in Castle Rock, Colorado at 7,495 yards. The high altitude, however makes balls travel 15-20% farther.

Q: What's the shortest?
A: Indian Wells in Palm Springs, California at only 6,478 yards.

Q: What's the easiest course on the tour?
A: Las Vegas Country Club, with an average score about three under par.

Q: What's the easiest hole?
A: The first hole at Las Vegas Country Club. A par-five, it recently had an average score of 4.261.

Q: So what's the hardest hole?
A: The par-four third hole at TPC Las Colinas (Texas), which averaged 4.587.

Q: How fast are the greens in a pro tournament?
A: Generally between 9 and 11 on the Stimpmeter, although Oakmont, Augusta National, and occasional U.S. Opens have been known to push 12. A Stimpmeter is a small, ramp-like device that rolls a golf ball at a given initial speed on a green. If the ball rolls ten feet, that green is rated a "10" on the Stimpmeter.

Handicaps of the Rich & Famous

 **HOW** *does your handicap rank with the rich & famous? Here's a variety of recent celebrity handicaps. (Note that baseball play- ers make great golfers.)*

Johnny Bench. . scratch	Michael Jordan 6	Craig T. Nelson 10
John Elway 2	Donald Trump . . . . 7 (b)	Mark McGwire 10
Mark Rypien. . . . . 2 (a)	Jim Palmer 7	Bobby Rahal 10
Mac Davis 2	Joe Namath 8	Dennis Quaid 10
Bill Lambier 3	Stan Smith 8	Roger Moore 10
Phil Simms 4	Smokey Robinson . . . 8	McLean Stevenson . .10
Maury Povich 4	Tom Candiotti 8	Peter Ueberroth 11
Orel Hershiser 4	Charles Barkley 8	Nelson Doubleday . . 11
Pete Dye 5	Ed Marinaro 9	Charles Schwab 11
Mike Schmidt 5	Frank Viola 9	George Brett 11
James Garner 6	Jim Morris 9	Bryant Gumbel 11
Steve Gatlin 6	Henry Kravis 9	Bernie Kosar 12
Dan Marino 6	Roger Clemens 9	Glen Campbell 12
Dan Quayle 6	Lawrence Taylor 10	Jim McMahon 12

Jack Nicholson 12	Bill Murray 16	Jack Lemmon . . . 20 (c)	(a) Rypien won the 1993 Pro Quarterback Pro Golf Challenge with partner Corey Pavin.
Tom Glavine 13	Tom Smothers 16	Brent Musburger . . . 20	
O.J. Simpson 13	Marvin Davis 16	Michael Keaton 20	
Bob Gibson 13	Sean Connery 17	Gene Hackman 20	(b) known to drop balls out of his trousers and refer to himself as "The Trumpster."
John Denver 15	Gerald Ford 17	George Bush 20	
Danny Sullivan 15	Leslie Nielsen 18	Robert Merrill 21	(c) Lemmon, despite his official 20, is possibly the worst avid celebrity golfer. Insiders estimate his actual handicap to be around 36. Despite years at the AT&T Celebrity Pro-Am, he has yet to make the cut. Double all bets.
Charles Schulz 15	Alan Shepherd 18	Lawrence Welk 24	
Jason Bateman 15	Don Johnson 18	Joe DiMaggio 25	
Huey Lewis 15	Paula Zahn 18		
Bill Clinton 16	Eddie Van Halen 19		
Joe Montana 16	Clint Eastwood 19		
Julius Irving 16	Bonnie Blair 20		
B.J. Thomas 16	Robert Loggia 20		
Cheryl Ladd 16	Joe Pesci 20		

CHAPTER 5

Golf Games That Don't Require a Golf Course (or Clubs, or Tees, or Balls...)

Shoe Golf

You don't need clubs, spikes, tees, or even a golf course for this one, because Shoe Golf involves tossing a shoe with your foot around a fabricated course. You can play indoors or out, multiple holes or cross country. Targets can be trees, lamp-posts, chairs, sleeping dogs, whatever.

Perhaps the best way to describe the game is to discuss the way we played it in boarding school, where we linksters would gather at night, donned in traditional garb. (Shoe Golf is a very formal sport.) The starting point was often the roof of a building on the far end of campus. The shoe of choice was the Topsider, and some players would wear a sneaker on their other foot for traction.

Once on the "tee," we would decide the layout of the first hole. Generally, the "pin" would be a person, usually someone we didn't like. "Let's play to Chet Farnsworth," a player would suggest. "Splendid!" another would reply in his best Gatsby voice. Whoever hit Chet Farnsworth in the fewest shoe "flings" won the hole. All pavement was con-sidered a hazard necessitating a drop and a one-stroke penalty, but everything else was in play.

The tricky part, of course, was this: Where was Chet? Was he in his room? In study hall? The chemistry lab? Most of us would start tossing toward his dorm at the other end of campus. However, there was usually one player who would decide to pursue a strategic gamble and toss in another direction. That posed a dilemma for his opponents: Did he have inside information? Was he bluffing? Should you follow?

Eventually, assuming we avoided campus authority figures (not always the case), we'd all find Chet. At this point, the formality of traditional golf was strictly observed. The players farthest away flung first. Time was granted to align shots. Clever *bon mots* were exchanged. All the while, no one would say anything to poor, clueless Chet, who was pretty sure we were having fun at his expense but couldn't figure out exactly how. He was especially bewildered if he was buck-naked in the shower when we found him.

Once Chet was played out, we would agree on a new hole, perhaps a lawn sculpture we didn't like or a professor's car. The point was, mainly, to be a smart ass. Of course, off campus, in the real world, such behavior is usually interpreted by casual observers as a bad case of arrested adolescence, so don't say you weren't warned. 🏌

Frisbee Golf

Another popular campus pursuit, Frisbee Golf's rules are the same as Shoe Golf's, except there are usually no hazards. Also, targets more conventional than actual people are preferable.

Design a course that uses the available geography. It can be a local park, a pedestrian mall, whatever. Simply designate nine or 18 targets—trees, lampposts, mail boxes, benches, sleeping dogs—and play to them with Frisbees. Challenge players with holes that require different throwing styles. Make some holes long and some short. Have some bend around a corner or travel over water. Make a hole that offers a short, narrow route for the daring or a long, easy route for the timid. Use your imagination. (Note: Some public parks actually have permanent Frisbee-target layouts. Alexandria, Virginia, for example, has a fine course.)

Many people especially enjoy playing Frisbee Golf at night with glow-in-the-dark models. 🏌

Tennis Golf

We played this one all the time as kids, but it's fun at any age. You'll need two or three acres of space, preferably cluttered with trees, sheds, gardens, and other obstacles.

Design a course with as many holes (up to 18) as possible. The emphasis should be on making them fun and eccentric. Try to find risk/reward situations, where daring players can shave strokes. The holes themselves can be anything stationary: trees, benches, bushes, and so forth.

When the course is laid out, play golf using a tennis ball and only one club. I always found a five- or six-iron to be the best choice. 🏌

Goose Tag

Okay, this isn't exactly a golf game, but it's damn entertaining. If you represent any radical wildlife organizations or whining animal rights groups, please read no further.

Ever get totally annoyed by the geese that litter your course? Ever wonder how they could possibly excrete twice their body weight in a single day? You're not alone. Though irritating, geese are great fun to harass. Try separating a gosling from its mother and watch how angry she gets. She'll hiss and flap her wings and act like she's going to charge you. Yeah, like you're really scared. Aside from the fact that you're #1 on the food chain, you have a six-iron in your hand with her name on it.

So, while wandering up the 16th hole at my home course on Long Island (one of the great geese-crapping grounds of the world), my partner and I decided to play a little goose tag. The object is simply to tap a goose with your club. I recommend using one of those Japanese drivers that weighs about two ounces and is 90-inches long—a light and versatile tool for the goose tagger. Successfully tagging a bird is a challenge but not impossible. Take a tip from that great predator of the Seren-geti, the cheetah: pick one target and stick with it until you've scored.

When you hear the noxious gaggle still squawking long after you've passed, you'll feel the satisfaction that comes from a job well done. Incidentally, double your points if you can tag a swan, and triple them if you get a mother with a cygnet (that's what baby swans are called).

Play Goose Tag as a Garbage game, if you want: one dollar for each goose tagged without delaying the game.

CHAPTER 6

Betting on Pro Tournaments

YES, THERE ARE GOLF GAMES you can play at the office or even as a total couch potato. These games involve betting on the fortunes of professional golfers. Try one some rainy Saturday afternoon. A ten-foot birdie putt by Jeff Sluman that, to say the least, you never before cared about will suddenly have you glued to the TV when it means twenty clams to you.

Ten Man

A fabulous format for betting on tournaments, Ten Man is best used for major events like the Masters. Two to six bettors alternately "draft" ten golfers each, with a roll of the dice deciding who picks first. These golfers become your "team." If you can't find a pre-tournament listing of the players, make the selections after the first round.

The performance of the golfers on each team determines who wins and loses money. The two-player version works as follows:

1. Pay a dollar for each cumulative stroke differential. Add your ten golfers' scores for all four rounds and compare it to your opponent's total score. Suppose your pros shot a total of 2,880, and your opponent's picks shot 2,910. You'd win $30. (If you picked a golfer who missed the cut, double his two-round score and add ten as a penalty.)

2. Pay a $10 bonus for
   - owning players who hold the lead after the first, second, or third rounds;

   - owning players shooting the low round during the second, third, or fourth rounds;

   - each player finishing in the top ten, excluding the winner.

3. Pay a $25 bonus for the winning golfer.

4. At the Masters, have a $10 side bet on the winner of the par-3 tournament on Wednesday.

As you can see, the stakes can really add up, so feel free to adjust them. This is especially true if you're playing with more than two bettors. With three to six bettors, when a bettor wins a category, all the others owe that player. For instance, suppose there are five bettors, and bettor #1 owns the golfer with the low round on the first day. Each of the other bettors owes bettor #1 $10. And for the cumulative score differential, each bettor owes the winner $1 times their own differential with the winner.

One hint: Golf is a streaky sport, so don't just pick the big names or consult an earnings list. Find out who's played well recently, and balance that against who's played well at that particular tournament in the past. Consider style of play, too. The British Open, for example, is played on links courses, which will often favor a low-ball hitter. The Masters favors long-ball hitters and good putters. The U.S. Open favors Scott Simpson. 🏌

Two (Three, or Four) Man

Divide the field of golfers into teams of two, three, or four so that the cumulative pre-tournament odds for each team are approximately the same. (*Golf Digest* and *Golf Magazine* occasionally print pre-tournament odds for the top players.) So, in the case of two-man teams, Greg Norman at 8-1 might be teamed with Corey Pavin at 40-1. Total odds: 48. Balance them against a team of, say, Paul

Azinger at 18-1 and Ken Green at 30-1. Divide all the players this way, and don't panic if it doesn't come out exactly; it won't.

After creating the teams, each bettor takes turns selecting one or more teams, either at random or straight from the list. Award $20 from each bettor to the bettor whose team contains the winning golfer. From there, you can create numerous other prizes. For example, add a penalty if none of a team's golfers makes the cut. See Ten Man for other ideas.

Sometimes, You Just Gotta Play

❑ At the Jinga Golf Course in Uganda, golfers are permitted free drops from hippopotami footprints and must yield to elephants.

❑ In a recent round at Pebble Beach, Bill Sadler, a Lieutenant Commander in the U.S. Navy, found that golf can be as punishing as pro football.

Sadler hit his tee shot on the famous eighth hole a bit to the right, and it trickled over the edge of the seaside cliff, coming to rest on a small ledge. When he reached down to retrieve his ball, the ground beneath him gave way, and he fell 140 feet and landed on a small patch of sand. Sadler escaped with a sprained ankle, a broken rib, and assorted cuts and bruises.

Has Sadler given up on golf? No, "just cliffs."

CHAPTER 7

Night Games

Closest to the Pin

In this game, players find their way in the darkness to a par three — usually the one nearest the clubhouse. Once on the tee, they have a simple closest-to-the-pin contest. The winner need not be on the green — but he must find his ball. Typically, this leads to the hilarious sight of grown-ups sniffing around the woods in the dark.

This game is best after a club dinner when everyone is more or less liquored-up. Over the years, there have been some fine matches held in the wee hours at courses such as the Garden City Golf Club on Long Island, which has the unique feature of a par three for its 18th hole, making the whole affair quite convenient.

Noted Greenwich sandbagger and night golf veteran Bill Sawch maintains that most people hit the ball fat when swinging in the dark, a supposition I have verified with any number of myopic flailings. Thus, he claims he has won a lot of money by purposefully trying to hit it thin. ✒●

Blind Man

Like Closest to the Pin, Blind Man is best played after one of those cigar-smoking, boozy club functions. Select one person to be the "Blind Man" and blindfold him thoroughly. Then, take him to a hole on the course, but don't let him know which one. Next, remove the flagstick from the hole.

Bring at least two escorts to prevent the Blind Man from wandering into water hazards or, if you're on a Pete Dye course, 30-foot bunkers. ▪●

Night Golf

Night Golf is the same as regular golf, but linksters play in the dark with a glow-in-the-dark ball. They are surprisingly easy to see, even at great distances, and they are actually easier to find than normal balls when you shank one in the cabbage. On a warm summer night, Night Golf makes for a memorable and fun diversion. ▪●

Once he's in the tee box, spin him around (remember "Pin the Tail on the Donkey"?) and tell him to find the hole. The other players bet that he can't find it in 30 minutes with the flag removed. (A variation: make it 15 minutes with the flag in.) Choose a hole that's a good test of the player's knowledge of the course.

GolFact

Many people state with authority that a golf shot with draw travels farther because it has topspin. In fact, it has no topspin at all. It simply possesses less backspin.

CHAPTER 8

The Practice Green

D
ID YOU KNOW THAT GOLFERS, regardless of handicap, tend to use about 40% of their strokes on the greens? But give most golfers ten minutes before a round, and they'll usually rush out and bang 20 balls with their driver as hard as they can. Golfers should always make some time for the practice green, because putting is the most overlooked part of the game.

The problem is, practicing putting isn't nearly as entertaining as launching cannons on the range. So, let's make the time on the practice green fun. Try betting some money on the following games. (I've always found that a wager can make even knitting interesting, but maybe that's just me.) Here are some ideas:

- Work on your long putts by playing closest to the hole, with the hole being 70 or 80 feet away. A two-putt is mandatory to win.

- Play a route to a hole around another hole, so that the best putt possible lips out and around the shorter hole (the "hazard" cup). Fewest strokes wins. Sinking your ball in the hazard hole earns a penalty stroke.

- Play an entire 18-hole Nassau in which the loser of each hole gets to declare the layout of the next. Be creative; we often hit from off the putting surface entirely. For instance, you might be playing to a hole that's only ten feet away,

EXPRESS GREEN 2 STROKES OR LESS

but before you may sink it you must first putt around — or bank it off — the clubhouse. (Note: It's a good idea to limit these more eccentric activities to times when members of the Greens Committee are nowhere in sight.)

- Have you ever seen some of the bizarre, twisted pieces of metal and graphite they try to pawn off as putters these days? Many look like rejects from *Star Trek*'s prop department. Here's your chance to try them. Play any of the above games but use different putters. Each player chooses his opponent's putter from the pro shop.

To add to the entertainment, try playing with sty-mies; players may not mark their balls, thus often blocking their opponents' paths to the hole. This is the way real men like C.B. MacDonald and Bobby Jones played in the olden days before, say, *Caddyshack*.

Richard Smith, the well-known Southern California cabbage pounder and strike-out artist, was once faced with both a stymie and a "hazard" hole to negotiate. His solution: pound a ricochet shot off the wall of the nearby pro shop. The ball came to rest about two feet from the target hole.

For a more formal practice green game, try…

Seven Point

Seven Point involves two or more players, each trying to get seven points first. After they select a hole, players gain points as follows:

- sinking the putt when no one else does: 2 points

- closest to the hole when no one sinks the putt: 1 point

- three-putt: negative 3 points

The first player to reach seven points wins and is paid based on the difference in point totals. If there's a tie, play until someone with seven or more points has at least a one-stroke lead over everyone else.

Honors on each hole goes to the highest point winner from the preceding hole. Play with stymies to make the game especially interesting. 🎙●

Horse

In this version of the age-old schoolyard basketball game, one player putts to a hole of his choice. If his opponent gets closer, player 1 earns an "H" and gets the honor on the next putt. If his opponent hits a worse putt, player 2 gets the "H." If both players sink the putt, no one gets a letter, and the order stays the same. Play out the holes until someone gets a "HORSE." 🎙●

> **"It has been observed that absolute idiots play the steadiest."**
> — **Sir Walter Simpson, The Art of Golf**

A Brief Golf Lexicon

Have trouble sounding like a pro at your last golf outing? Couldn't come up with better commentary than "Crummy shot, Roy"? Here are some good terms to memorize:

Shots

Banana: a big, looping slice.

Dart: a ball that flies high and sticks near the pin.

Dionne Warwick: a putt that slides, or "walks on by," the hole. Usually way by.

Elephant's Ass: a shot that's high—and stinks.

Fried Egg: a ball buried in a bunker.

Moonraker: a shot, often a drive, that has an high trajectory (a.k.a. "Rainmaker").

Oral Roberts: a shot hit off the heel (a "heeler," get it?).

Overfade: euphemism for a slice.

Ravi Shankar: a shank.

Snapper: a "snap" hook.

Sunriser: a drive that starts low but rises rapidly.

Teeth: what a ball with bite has, as in "That shot had teeth."

Worm Burner: a hard, topped shot that runs along the ground.

People

Alice: someone constantly leaving putts short (a.k.a. "Nancy").

Bandit: a golfer who consistently plays beneath his handicap; to be avoided (a.k.a. "Sandbagger," "Shark").

Cabbage Pounder: someone who spends a lot of time in the rough.

Chopper: someone who frequently hits it fat.

Pigeon: a golfer who never plays to his handicap; to be courted. Send limo to get him to the course, if necessary.

Places

Amateur Side: low side of the cup, when putting.

Brillo: the short rough surrounding a green. (Also a nickname for Bob Tway, after his curly coiffure.)

Brown Sugar: a bunker.

Chopping Mall: the metaphoric place one goes when having a horrible round.

Dance Floor: the putting green.

Hay: deep rough, usually gorse or heather.

Jail: bad rough, possibly out of bounds.

Oscar Brown: out of bounds.

Pro Side: high side of the cup, when putting.

Rockpile: the practice tee.

Soup: water.

CHAPTER 9

Games for the Locker Room

WE CERTAINLY COULDN'T call this *The Complete Book of Golf Games* and forget about the 19th hole—home of large cocktails and larger lies. Here, too, the gaming action can provide considerable amusement.

Basic Dice

The standard game used in most halfway houses and clubhouses to determine who buys the drinks has no name. It isn't particularly thrilling, but it is faster than other games and therefore preferable in time-constrained situations.

Players should "piddle" (roll one die) to see who rolls first. The object is to get the most of a kind, using five dice, in the fewest number of roles. Player 1 may use up to three rolls but may quit on the first or second roll if he thinks his "hand" is strong enough. Subsequent rollers are then limited to the same number of rolls. Like poker, much of the strategy lies in whether to hold or try for a better hand.

All 1's are wild, and a roll of five 6's is the best possible hand. And, obviously, five 6's achieved in fewer than three rolls is even stronger. Players may keep any dice they want after each roll and then play the rest. The high hand each round is excused from the competition, and the others' dice start over.

Pig

My personal favorite clubhouse game, which has an on-course variation (see page 37), Pig is a game of minimalist beauty. Pig requires two dice, one pencil, and one sheet of paper. The object of the game is to be the first player to accumulate over 100 points by repeatedly rolling the dice. On each turn, a player may roll as long as he wishes, with two exceptions:

• The player rolls a 1 on either die. When this happens, the player loses all his points on that turn and forfeits the dice.

• The player rolls double 1's. In this case, the player loses all the points he's accumulated for the entire game.

The typical strategy is to accumulate a reasonable number of points, usually 20-25, and then "bank" them by passing the dice to the next player. Players who try for too many points in one roll risk living up to the game's name, at which point it's

appropriate for everyone to snort and squeal, a la *Deliverance*.

Two more rules:

• You can't quit on doubles (except double 1's).

• Once a player goes over 100, all the other players must have a chance to match his score. If another player catches him, everyone gets a chance to catch player #2, and so on. This way, no one is ever out of the game until everyone is out except the winner.

By the way, the pencil and paper is for the scorekeeper. Make sure it's someone who can actually add.

Don't let the simplicity of Pig fool you. It's rife with strategy and amusement. So the next time you have an uncontrollable urge to play backgammon, try using the table for Pig instead. 🖊

The traditional Scottish names for the clubs we use every day:

driver — play club	3-iron — mid-mashie
2-wood — brassie	4-iron — mashie iron
3-wood — spoon	5-iron — mashie
4-wood — cleek	6-iron — spade mashie
5-wood — baffy	7-iron — mashie niblick
7-wood — ginty	8-iron — pitcher/lofter
1-iron — driving iron	9-iron — niblick
2-iron — mid-iron	

Twenty-Four

Yet another dice game, the initial object of Twenty-Four is to roll as high a number in five rolls as possible. Player 1 roles five dice and removes at least one—and as many as five. The idea is to remove the highest dice. He continues until he has rolled five times or has removed all the dice. His total is then always decreased by 24 points. If he rolls 26, then 26-24 equals 2, so 2 becomes that player's "point."

Next, that same player rolls all five dice again with the goal of rolling the same number as his point. If the point is 2 and he rolls two 2's, he puts those dice aside and rolls the remaining three, hoping for more 2's. He keeps rolling until he misses his point entirely or has succeeded in getting five 2's. (A player misses his point when he rolls and none of the dice matches the point.) A roll of five 2's is worth ten points (5 times 2), a roll of four 2's is worth eight points, and so on. If the player fails to roll any 2's (or whatever his point was), he gets 0 points and passes the dice. (The most points possible is 30, achieved when a player's point is 6 and he rolls five 6's.) Since each point is a betting unit (typically $1.00), things can add up.

Getting 0 points is not necessarily bad, because it's possible to have a negative point. This happens when the opening rolls add up to less than 24. If you roll 20, for example, your point is -4. If you then roll three more 4's, your score is -12. Note: You may not stop rolling as long as you keep rolling your point. So, if you start with a negative point, you hope to avoid your point and pass the dice with a 0 and a smile.

Finally, rolling a 24 on your first throw gives you an automatic 0. Pass the dice. ▰●

Maidstone

This game was concocted on a miserable day on eastern Long Island when we were rained out but insisted on hanging around the locker room for half the afternoon.

Player #1 rolls five dice up to three times, removing, as in Twenty-Four, any dice he chooses after each roll. The goal is to roll the highest total number possible, 30 being tops (5 times 6). Player #1 may choose to stop rolling after his first or second roll if he thinks his hand is strong enough. The advantage in this is that it limits the succeeding players to this number of rolls as well. In general, the object is to avoid being the low man for each round.

The next player's objective is to tie or beat player #1's score, and thus avoid being the low man. If he feels like screwing the players who haven't rolled yet, he may elect to try to run the score beyond what is strictly necessary. This includes cutting the number of rolls allowed. For example, if player #1 rolls 20 in three rolls and player #2 has 21 in two rolls, he may stop there and thereby limit other players to two rolls.

The low man drops out after each round until one person, the winner, remains. Start each round with someone new, since going early is an advantage. Each player puts a specified amount in the hat, winner take all. Also, anyone rolling a total of 5 in their allotted number of rolls must throw another unit into the hat. ▰●

Where the Big Dogs Eat

Here, for no particular reason, is a list of the longest holes in the world:

Par	Yards to green	Yards per shot*	Hole	Club
3	270**	270	16	International Golf Club, Bolton, MA***
4	500	250	6	Eisenhower Golf Club, Industry City, CA
5	710	237	17	Palmira Golf and Country Club, St. John's, IN
6	747	187	17	Black Mountain Golf Course, Black Mountain, NC
7	948	190	6	Koolan Island Golf Club, Australia

*An exclusive, you-heard-it-here-first calculation.

**Golf standards dictate that par-three holes shouldn't be longer than 250 yards, and par-fours not longer than 470 yards. Sometimes, however, prevailing conditions of grade, wind, or altitude result in the decision to build longer holes. Also, as golf equipment improves, standards will change.

*** The International Golf Club, at 8,290 yards (par 77), claims to be the longest course in the world.

GolFact

At one golf club in Rhodesia, it was business as usual during those annoying little uprisings in the early 1970's. The club simply amended its rules to allow for the replay of a stroke if interrupted by gunfire or a "sudden explosion." Presumably, if the explosion wasn't sudden, the stroke counted.

I Want More!

I F, DURING YOUR FORAYS into the great golf outdoors, you hear about or invent any games not included in this book, please let me know about them. Also, if you have variations or comments on the games I've described, I'd like to hear from you as well.

If we get enough new games, we'll create a sequel, and if we use your game in the sequel, we'll send you a free copy! Send your letters to

> Scott Johnston
> Golf Research Dept.
> Mustang Publishing
> P.O. Box 3004
> Memphis, TN 38173 USA

(Game descriptions become the property of Mustang Publishing. Though your contribution is not tax deductible, it could give you a measure of literary immortality.)

More Great Books from Mustang Publishing

Lucky Pants & Other Golf Myths by Joe Kohl. From drawings that poke fun at the myths all duffers hold dear to illustrations that skewer the foibles of the golf-obsessed, this collection of over 80 witty golf cartoons deserves a place of honor on every golfer's bookshelf. *"Hilarious!"—Fore Florida.* **$7.95**

The Complete Book of Beer Drinking Games by Andy Griscom, Ben Rand, & Scott Johnston.With over 500,000 copies sold, this book reigns as the imbiber's bible! From descriptions of classic beer games like Quarters and Blow Pong to hilarious new contests like Slush Fund and Beer Hunter—plus lots of funny cartoons, essays, and lists— this book remains the party essential. *"The 'Animal House' of literature."—Dallas Morning News.* **$8.95**

Beer Games 2: The Exploitative Sequel by Griscom, Rand, Johnston, & Balay. With over 40 new games from around the world, plus the wild "Beer Catalog," this sequel is even funnier than the original. If you liked the first book, you'll love **Beer Games 2**!
"Simply awesome."—The Vermont Cynic. **$8.95**

The Hangover Handbook by Nic van Oudtshoorn. Face it—if you bought the "Beer Games" books, you'll _need_ this one, too. A humorous and practical guide to curing morn-ing-after woes, this book boasts over 100 hangover reme-dies from ancient to modern times, plus hilarious drinking trivia. *"A drinker's best friend."—Clemson Tiger.* **$8.95**

Europe for Free by Brian Butler. If you're traveling Europe on a tight budget— or if you just love a bargain— this is the book for you. Describing thousands of free things to do and see all over Europe, this book will save you lots of lira, francs, and pfennigs. *"Well-organized and packed with ideas."—Modern Maturity.* **$10.95**

Also in this series:
London for Free by Butler. **$9.95**
DC for Free by Butler. **$9.95**
Hawaii for Free by Carter. **$9.95**
The Southwest for Free by Edwards. **$9.95**
Paris for Free (Or Extremely Cheap) by Beffart. **$10.95**

Mustang books should be available in your local book-store. If not, send a check or money order for the price of the book— plus $3.00 shipping *per book*— to Mustang Publishing, PO Box 3004, Memphis, TN 38173 USA. To order by credit card, call toll-free 800-250-8713 (or 901-521-1406). *International orders:* Please pay in U.S. funds, and add $5.00 to the total for Air Mail shipping.